SOUL INSURANCE

My life's research Testimony of how Lord Jesus saved me from this world

Kaustav Chowdhury

BlueRose Publishers
NewDelhi • London

First Published in December 2021

ISBN: 978-93-93388-53-7

BLUEROSE PUBLISHERS
www.bluerosepublishers.com
info@bluerosepublishers.com
+91 8882 898 898

Cover Design:
Geetika Kandari
Typographic Design:
Pooja Sharma

Distributed by: BlueRose, Amazon, Flipkart

"Declare His glory among the nations, His wonders among all people."

Psalm 96:3

Disclaimer

The author is offering this book and the content based on the data collected from his observed research, and makes no forced representations of any kind of worldviews written in this book onto the readers. The author disclaims that there might be a few topics or images that might make some readers uncomfortable. In addition, the publisher and the author assume no responsibility for errors, inaccuracies, omissions, or any other inconsistencies herein.

The content of this book is for **informational purposes only** and is not intended to accuse, brainwash, or bring any sort of violence on any religious group, individual, creed or sect. Upon reading this book, you might stumble upon something that is offensive to your existing beliefs or controversial in your worldview. The author requests each one of the readers to keep an open mind and review its content in an unbiased mindset.

All this book shows is the collection of data, the author has researched and his personal experiences regarding God, religion, demons and other related topics that affect us all. Please act on your own Free Will while making any major decision regarding any suggestions and recommendations given in this book. After-all, all human beings are free to make their own decisions.

The testimony and examples narrated in this book show such results, which may not apply to an average reader, and are not intended to represent or guarantee that you will experience similar results.

The continuation in reading this book implies the reader's acceptance of this disclaimer.

Introduction

Have you done your soul insurance?

I have seen people doing their life insurance. Constantly worrying about what will happen to their loved ones and their earthly properties after they die. Will they have enough money to sustain themselves? Will they fall for something and never recover financially? Will their assets fall into the wrong hands? So many worries in this carnal life.

But what about your soul?

I strongly believe that your soul is one of its kind and it lives on forever and ever. Your fleshly body will rot and everything that is carnally built will fall one day. They are finite and have an expiration date tagged on them. It's just a matter of time that they will perish. Some sooner, some later. But first, let me introduce myself.

Hello World. I am Kaustav Chowdhury and I am a born again soul in Christ Jesus. I used to hate Christians in my youthful days, but now I am myself a born again Christian, working for the Lord's Kingdom. I am writing this book to share my testimony of how Lord Jesus saved me from the evils of this world, opened my eyes, and showed me its inner workings. How facts can back up your faith with a little research and can clear many unanswered questions I had during my childhood days.

I have procrastinated since I was baptized in His **Holy Spirit** and have gone through great spiritual warfare in order to complete this book. But finally, the book is here for you. We are called to glorify His mighty name. Even writing this testimony is a means of glorifying

Jesus and His coming Kingdom. I am offering this book to all who are willing to read and seek the truth.

Those who have an ear to hear let them all hear...

My motto was to take all the research content that I did as an unbeliever and to write my testimony in such a way that anyone who reads this, can relate to it at every step. I used all my designing and writing experience to creatively narrate my story so as to show exactly what I want you to know.

Through the contents of this book, I have tried to show how I started my research journey of knowing the truth, backing all my findings with logic, history, and going deep into the rabbit hole. Digging up how this world is operated and what is wrong at its core. I want to give you an advance warning before you start reading this book. Some might find these contents offensive. There is no doubt about it. To them, I would advise to have an open mind and see what I have to say till the end. **It was offensive to me as well when I was doing my research.**

I have also tried to keep the language as grounded as possible. My observations on all these topics will be valuable and let it be a part of your thought process as well. I am just showing you the data I collected and where it led me.

I pray that each one of us born-again believers, whoever has a unique testimony to share, let this book be an inspiration for you to share your Testimony as well. Kindly share the observations of this book with all your friends and family.

...

Acknowledgement

Completing this book was not easy as I had to be in constant spiritual battles to do so. I would like to express my deep gratitude to my sister, parents and my Pastor for their patience, guidance, encouragement and constant useful critiques of this research work over the months that I was writing it.

I would also like to thank all the YouTube channels, online resources, Reverends, Pastors, brothers in Christ, Biblical scholars, and book authors who have helped me to seek the truth. You guys are anointed. Without your precious content, quotes and guidance, it would have been impossible for me to get this worldview that I am going to share in this book.

A special thank you to Ernest Griset for his illustration, Brother Mathew Sammie, and Ray Comfort for providing resources that have helped in building parts of my research. The book would not have turned out the way it did if your contributions were not added.

I would also like to extend my gratitude to my publishers for walking with me on every step in the publishing process. You guys are awesome.

Finally, I would like to thank the **Holy Spirit** and my Lord and Savior **Jesus Christ,** because of whom I went through this transformation and this research began. I started my journey in seeking the truth and finally ended up on Him. I dedicate this entire book to Him and His will.

Let us begin.

Contents

"Behold, a sower went out to sow. And as he sowed, some seed fell by the wayside; and the birds came and devoured them. Some fell on stony places, where they did not have much earth; and they immediately sprang up because they had no depth of earth. But when the sun was up they were scorched, and because they had no root they withered away. some fell among thorns, and the thorns sprang up and choked them. But others fell on good ground and yielded a crop: some a hundredfold, some sixty, some thirty. He who has ears to hear, let him hear!"

Matthew 13: 3 - 9

Sowing Of Seeds

God has inspired me to follow Him in many ways, not just when I was little, but at every stage of my growing life. As a normal kid who had lots of curiosity, I had asked countless questions to my parents about life, God, the purpose of our existence, how this happens or how that happens etc... All these deep questions have been left unanswered to my disappointment, and I have been told not to ask such questions again.

I believe that as parents, they themselves don't have any answers to my questions. I believe when they were little kids, they also had similar curiosity about life and purpose, but they might have been told by their parents not to ask such questions, or they would get punished for being so curious.

All children from any generation deep questions out of innocence and their curiosity dilutes over time because they don't get any reasonable answers for adults. You would agree on this with me, right?

I had a good fear of God and His judgment, regardless of my awareness of who, or what "God" even meant. There are many incidents in my life that highlight that fear.

Let me share one such incident.

This happened in my school when I was in my 2nd standard. I was sitting on the last bench and it was a free period as the respective teacher was absent that day. A substitute teacher was assigned for our class who just came to keep the class quiet and fill in the time.

I was very bored as there was nothing for me to do. So to just pass time, I remember picking and torturing an ant for fun and eventually killing it. I was just having fun and that act did not bother me.

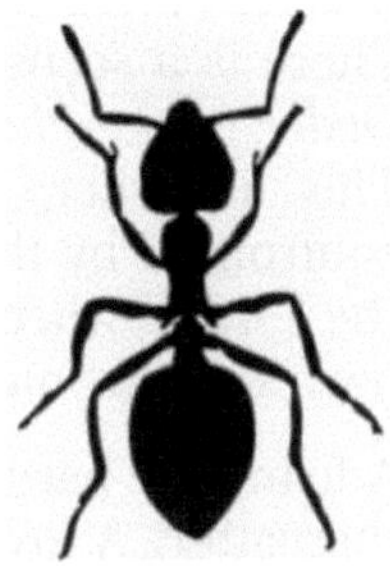

Once the ant died, I suddenly realized deep inside of me that I had done something bad. It was written in my heart somehow that murdering animals and having fun doing so was wrong.

This realization became even stronger when a classmate of mine, who was sitting in front of me, pointed that out. The fear of God came over me, and I was frightened that this deed of mine would be bad in the eyes of the one who is the Creator of this Universe. I was in tears and immediately asked for His genuine forgiveness.

I prayed, or more accurately, pleaded with God not to punish me for that mistake. I was crying by the time my prayer ended. Unknowingly out of my innocence, I learned to genuinely repent to God that day.

Now, when I think about it, I can see God was teaching me so many little but important things through many of such encounters.

The Spark

Likewise, I recall back vividly when God first planted His seed in my heart before I knew what ***sin*** was. That spark began my heart's slow but steady transformation till the journey of my salvation.

This encounter involves a movie plot in which God used to reveal the desire in me of doing the right thing. There is a scene in the movie: *"Harry Potter and the Order of the Phoenix"*, known as the Order's entrance. This is where the evil witches and wizards are confronted by the good witches and wizards known as the 'Order' when Harry was about to surrender. If you have seen the movie, you would know.

A fearsome battle begins among the two wizard groups thereafter. A great visual of Good vs. Evil begins. The good ones were depicted in white and the evil ones in black.

I was in my 10th grade when I first saw that movie and the CGI and visual effects blew my mind. It was the year 2007 and we had never seen such great visuals before. I related to the good witches and wizards instantly. That scene was full of CGI fights as well, and the visuals gave me a perfect lens to see how the victory of good always happens over evil.

There were many other awesome fight scenes in that movie too, but the one I just described was engraved in my mind like no other. I often saw myself as one of those characters in the mirror. Someone who would make dramatic entrances; someone who would fight evil witches and rescue innocent people.

Movies like these do have such effects on kids.

That scene alone ignited a spark in me to search for the truth and do what is right and be on the good side of the battle. I loved it so much that I wanted to be a part of that group (someone who fights for good).

There are several issues with witches and wizards and them casting spells. I will discuss that in details later in the book, but at that time it was a mere inspiration for a teenager from a movie, and nothing more.

But now that I look back, I see that motivation as a gift from Jesus. Sowing a mindset that will bring me to Him years later as a harvest of a seed that falls on the ***good ground***.

Any form of witchcraft and wizardry is evil. There is no such thing as a good witch / wizard.

More on that later.

My Attitude towards Christians

I was born and raised in a small industrial city called Bokaro Steel City in the state of Jharkhand, India.

Since I was a boy, I used to hate Christians. Not Jesus, but Christians who were lukewarm and were only professing Christians. There were 2 main reasons.

The 1st reason was that I truly believed Christianity was the religion of the Britishers. The Brits had ruled over our land for centuries. And I believed they brought a foreign religion called Christianity to our land. It was the religion of the white man and they had this evil plan to make the whole world Christian and make everyone follow their religious beliefs. That is what I ignorantly believed.

A religion which is foreign and not of our own.

The 2nd reason I hated Christians was for an agenda that they had. In our locality, there were few Roman Catholic Priests who used to offer money to many poor communities in our city of Bokaro, and used to almost bribe them to come to their Churches. Throwing money at financially poor people to convert them to Christianity and fill their Church seats was their agenda and I had a strong disgust for that.

I even hated it more when one day, our maid started going to Church because she was bribed into doing so. I was in 12th standard then. We know it because she told that to my mother one day. She was not a born again soul, and neither did she personally know Jesus or what He had done on the cross. Not one bit.

So now instead of going to a temple, she was attending a Sunday church. Instead of wearing an Om necklace, she was wearing a cross necklace. Only the name of her religion and her temple changed, not her soul. She was basically the same spiritually.

What happened then, raised many questions in my furious mind. Questions like why God has created so many religions? If God is the same God for all religions, why then misguide people with different rules and all? Why can't God remove all religious beliefs that divide us and bring us under one unified belief?

I am a Hindu boy because I was born in India and was raised by a Hindu Family. Hypothetically, if I was born in Saudi Arabia, I would have definitely been a Muslim, or in Japan, I would have practiced Taoism. These were some bold and rage-filled questions that I had. And I knew my parents could not answer them. They would have told me to not ask such questions. So I kept all that frustration within me.

These questions were way beyond my league at the time. The answers to which came to me years later.

“How can you say, ‘We are wise,
And the law of the Lord is with us’?
But behold, the lying pen of the scribes
Has made it into a lie.”

Jeremiah 8:8

Year 2016

Fast-forward many years and it was 2015. My college was completed the previous year and I started working in Navi Mumbai. This year was very dark for me as I just came out of a demonic oppression. At that time, I didn't know that.

It was mostly incidents that happened with me in Navi Mumbai because a person whom I thought to be a very dear friend of mine back-stabbed me. I considered him my brother.

We were living together in the same apartment as we both worked in the same company as engineers, and it took a little time for me to realize that I was being manipulated, used upon, and was just working like a mechanical tool. I was not very happy with my 9-5 job either. I was gasping for some inner-peace.

Once I fully realized what the issue was, I immediately took the first opportunity to leave the company and that whole world that I had created to come back to my hometown. It was December of 2015.

For the very 1st time in my life, I was directionless and also jobless as I had no jobs lined up in front of me. I am the kind of person who plans and keeps a backup for any possible outcomes that could happen, even for the tiniest issues. Taking logical steps, one at a time. But this time, I was without a plan. The New Year 2016 started, but I had no idea what to do. A big question mark was hanging in front of me.

What will I do?

Though, I got that immediate doze of inner-peace, but it was short-lived. I had left my previous job in

Mumbai. I fled from there and came back to my hometown of Kolkata. For quite a while, I was at the mercy of my parents.

This was the moment when my pride in myself was completely shattered. My shoulders were too weak to carry this mess. The "*I can handle this all on my own*" attitude had completely vanished and I was left depressed.

I felt worthless because I was not earning money at that time, but mostly because I was mainly heartbroken because one of my dearest friends had back-stabbed me. Who can I trust now?

Recovering out of this was not what I knew could be done with my own strength. Time was plenty and there was nothing much I had to do. Now that I was broke and had a lot of free time, I wanted to utilize these moments somehow and so was motivated subconsciously to find an answer to all of my philosophical questions I had asked myself for so many years.

The soil of my heart was ready to nurture the seed of my old curiosities. A perfect time that God intended to grow in me, that seed which He planted almost 10 years ago.

?

If you were to die today, where would you go? Heaven or Hell?

The Question

In 2016, I was broke and so had a lot of spare time in my hand. Researching about deep philosophical topics on YouTube was growing as an addiction in me, so I thought to use it to my advantage.

Today, if you are having any good intellectual question or want to dig into anything deeper, the internet is the best solution for you. No doubt.

Honestly, the internet is a weird place. It is a mixture of all sorts of information that you can learn and benefit from. You will find some really awful stuff; some misleading stuff; some half-truths and some pure gold stuff.

But how will you identify the gold stuff?

It is you, who has to go through tons and tons of this stuff to identify that gold or gem information to hold on to develop your worldview. You should cross-verify a topic from 3 or more sources and link all the details to make a factual point.

Something that is closest to the truth and not biased information. The data that compels your mind to think on your own, to make wise decisions, and not to blindly adopt any information without verifying them aptly with other available sources.

As days went by, I was getting better at researching on various topics over the internet. In today's data-driven world, researching online can become a very high demand skillset in the marketplace.

As YouTube recommendations go, one day I stumbled upon a video that asked a very compelling question of me. I knew this question was it.

The question simply asked: "**If you were to die today, where would you go? Heaven or Hell?**"

This question has really made a lot of lost souls think twice about their salvation. For me personally, it really made me think more deeply than any other question. It grew in me within a week. This thought kept bugging my conscience.

Where will I go after I die? I had no answer to that question. It felt very offensive to me. I tried my best to forget it, but something in me kept bringing this question to my mind all the time.

Well, I am a good person. Am I not? Of course, I am headed towards Heaven. Why not? Does Heaven really exist? Is there any evidence of Heaven or Hell anyways? Or will I sleep forever after I am dead? What absurd questions right?

Who in their sane mind would want to go to hell? And by any chance, if someone comes to know that they are walking towards hell, will they not immediately change their way in the opposite direction?

I was asking these questions to myself. Till then, I believed anyone who lived a good life, did good deeds goes straight to heaven after they die. No questions asked. Just your good deeds must be more than your bad deeds, and you are all set for heaven. People like Hitler, Stalin, and Changez Khan, who have killed millions, are the ones who deserve Hell. They must rot in Hell. Not you. We definitely are way better people than them and so we will never, ever go to hell.

I know many of you reading now; think pretty much the same way. Right?

I was compelled to start researching this or else it would keep bugging me for the rest of my life. I had to answer that question anyhow. Will I, for sure go to heaven after I die? Is it 100% guaranteed? What if I go to hell?

I was not sure if I was going to heaven or not. I needed full confirmation. I was broke and had no work, so yeah... let the quest for this answer be my purpose for now. Had no idea what I was about to find.

God had been setting these circumstances in my life like a series of dominos. This question was the 1st domino to fall, starting the rest of the series to fall ahead.

I was hooked and planned to dig deeper.

"And you will seek Me and find Me when you search for Me with all your heart."

Jeremiah 29:13

Phase 1 Research

If I were to tell you that I am a black Swedish woman who lives on the planet Jupiter and commutes to Mars for my work of mining stardust, would you believe me? Will you offend me with the Truth, or will you let me be in my own ignorance?

I may also believe that you owe me $1,000,000,000 in cash and I need the payment today ASAP. Will you agree to that and pay me the full amount?

It's my belief. It's my version of the truth. How dare you not believe in it? Shut up and comply. Will you just nod to whatever I said or would you give me a tight slap and tell me to come to my senses?

Unfortunately, many live in similar confusions every day in this information age. It may not be as ridiculous as the above two examples that I shared, but people hold on to many beliefs which are not based on facts but purely on false information and emotions. These are the people who took the misleading stuff from the internet thinking it to be gold.

Believing whatever my emotions tell them to believe, mixed with loads of half-truths is what I wanted to avoid for my investigation. **I wanted to know the truth.** Will I be offended with what I find? Yes, of course I will. But will that stop me in my research? I hope it does not.

Falling for whatever is convenient as per our worldview is easy, but it keeps us in darkness, all the time. The darkness of not knowing the truth. Many people cannot handle the truth very well. They get emotional over their beliefs and harden their heart to whatever they have known to believe. If it's not their emotions, then cultural traditions and worldly pleasures are there to do that job. Proper digging regardless of how you feel is essential for everyone.

Researching on things you truly want to discover is easier than ever. What is stopping you? I suppressed my ego and my worldview to sit in the back seat and ***let Truth take me wherever it led.*** The only principle I had was to have no biased view on any thought or belief.

This was important to consider because today's information is mainly controlled in a specific narrative. The global mainstream media and social media have their own dark agenda to control our thought process. I definitely need to avoid false information or any individual's biased opinion. Because the last thing I want to have in my research is biased opinions disguised as facts by some so-called 'expert'.

Total Unbiased Truth

After-all, what could go wrong? There is nothing for me to lose. I will just stand like an umpire and observe everything neutrally. If I stumble on something great, I can just add it to my worldview, and anything offensive will go straight into my intellectual dustbin. A great mindset to start the Phase 1 journey.

"My people are destroyed for lack of knowledge..."

Hosea 4:6

Knowledge is Power

We have heard about this quote a lot of times but have hardly spent any time thinking deeply about it. Knowledge is the power to all who actually ask the right questions and start finding solutions with no biased presumptions. The journey that we take in researching gives us knowledge. It gives us the dots to connect. Dots that will create a big picture that can only be created if you connect all the dots over time. That big picture will certainly give you perspective on things that you didn't have before.

This might not be the textbook definition of knowledge, but this is how I have come to gain knowledge on many topics.

Out of the Comfort zone

From the beginning itself, I was placed outside of my comfort zone. I had no prior knowledge of any of the matter before my research that I am writing in this book.

The major topic that the Holy Spirit led me to before revealing Himself was about signs and symbols, witchcraft, celebrities selling their souls for fame; control over printing money. How secret societies run global banking systems. How dark principalities rule this world, etc...etc...

These are the principalities that control the laws, trades, war, world governments, and in general, the whole world's regulations.

I approached this by looking into many testimonials of industry veterans and their interviews of what they themselves have confessed. And trust me, there are many such videos of Hollywood stars all over the internet. It is up to you if you want to look into them. Let this be an activity for you.

The first topic that I will cover in my research is 'Symbols'.

Activity

Search for interviews and video testimonials of veteran rock stars, current pop singers, Hollywood actors and celebrities where they confess by themselves that they have sold their souls for fame and money.

"And have no fellowship with the unfruitful works of darkness, but rather EXPOSE them."

Ephesians 5:11

Symbols

To understand the world we live in, we have to know the signs and symbols surrounding us. Symbols are a method of communicating an idea without saying a single word. Today, symbols are placed everywhere without us knowing what they mean or what agenda they represent.

The more we see these symbols and do not understand them, or are ignorant about their actual meaning, the easier we adopt them in our everyday lifestyle unknowingly. The backdrop of this is that many times, our own lack of knowledge on these signs and symbols leads us indirectly to be a part of an agenda, cult, or religion without us being aware of them.

These symbols can be seen in hand signs, icons, logos, artworks, and literally in any sort of visual description.

This is what a Freemason [a member of an international order established for mutual help and fellowship, which holds elaborate secret ceremonies] has to say about symbols.

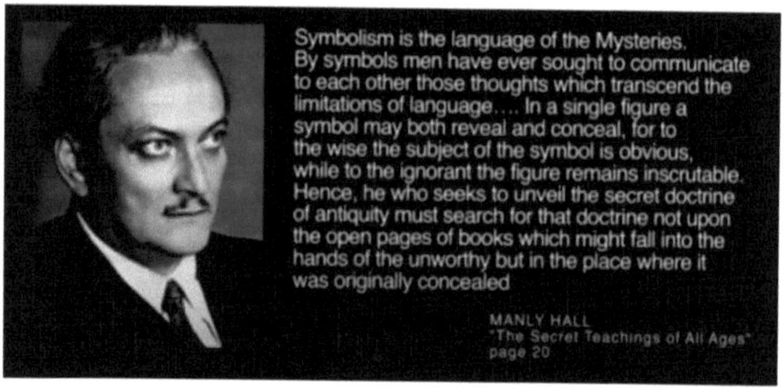

Symbols are obvious to those who know their meaning, but it is impossible for the ignorant to understand or interpret them. Once you start investigating and studying about **secret societies, cults, pagan civilizations, and mystery religions,** you will understand how symbols are used for centuries to communicate on every part of this planet, making this world more wicked and how far we has moved towards darkness.

Wake up. Be aware of these things.

For all the symbols that I am going to discuss here, we will dig up their origins, which are mostly connected to occult mysteries. Things that were done in secret are now done in plain sight, often covered in the name of comedy, entertainment, music videos, and reality shows.

Their main motto behind this is to make you subconsciously neutral so that you become desensitized to these symbols being around you all of the time.

The entire reason for me to write this book is to educate you and teach you what the Holy Spirit has revealed to me so that you can learn it yourself and teach it to your children, family, and friends and know what you have to avoid in life.

There are many symbols for us to look into. But for the length of this book, I will only discuss what are the most common symbols that are used to deceive us. I will not make this a lecture on symbolism. Trust me.

But before we go into detail, you have to know the characteristics of these symbols.

The 1st thing you have to know about symbols is that you cannot change the meaning of a symbol according to your understanding or likeness. If a symbol was originally created to portray or communicate a specific message, it doesn't matter what you decide that you want to use that symbol for. The original meaning of that symbol has not changed. It still means what it was always meant to mean.

Let us take an example.

You cannot take a pentagram symbol and all of a sudden claim it to represent Jesus. In your heart, you might truly believe this to be Jesus's symbol, but to the rest of the world, it will still mean a pentagram. And the pentagram represents black magic and witchcraft.

So the meaning of that symbol didn't change just because you wanted to rename it. Instead of seeing Jesus, others will see Satan and black magic because that is what the symbol means. No matter how pure your intentions are, you are only deceiving yourself and anyone who is getting influenced by you.

I took this example because the pentagram is considered an unholy symbol universally and can be easily identified. Again, you cannot change the meaning of a symbol, no matter how noble your intentions are.

The 2nd thing about symbolism is dangerous not mainly to our conscious mind but to our **subconscious mind**. We are not capable of guarding our subconscious mind. It just absorbs what it sees automatically. The subconscious is constantly collecting information and is storing it. A Bollywood movie called *Karthik calling Karthik* explains it perfectly, where the main character speaks to himself via phone calls and gives solutions to himself for all his problems because his subconscious mind has collected all the solutions that his conscious mind was looking for.

The kingdom of darkness and the ones following it know this very fact nicely. That is why they give subliminal messages through many social mediums, ads, posters, music, movies etc... To manipulate your subconscious to make you slowly comply with their agenda and changes they want to bring globally.

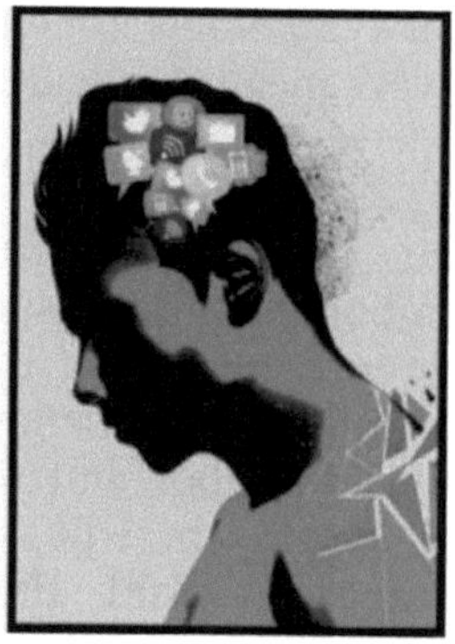

That is why big businesses try to target our subconscious with their ads. Advertising agencies hire psychologists and spend millions of dollars on them. They constantly research how the human mind works and how it can be manipulated to what they are promoting.

Subliminal means below the threshold of sensation or consciousness, perceived by or affecting someone's mind without their awareness of it. So you constantly see these messages throughout days, weeks, months, maybe years.

In this way, they are communicating a message that we are seeing all the time but don't know what is really happening.

When I was researching all of these. My mind was not only blown away, but I was able to relate to all the things I had experienced since I was little that were subliminal. Looking back, I was joining the dots that eventually made clear sense when all these truths appeared in front of me all of a sudden.

Hope you have got a basic idea of what these symbols are going to be. Let us begin with them in detail.

The All Seeing Eye

This symbol is one of the most common symbols, and it comes in many forms. This symbol is on the back of the one-dollar bill. A very common symbol flashed by celebrities, pop stars, etc... They constantly display it. It is basically just one eye and people show this by covering their one eye with their hand.

Sometimes it is a single eye in a pyramid (back of a dollar bill) or is just presented as a single eye. One eye that celebrities show by putting their hand on the other eye in all creative ways. It is such an awkward pose to make.

One eye symbolism in magazine

There is a complete collage dedicated to celebrities making the one eye-hand sign on the next page. I am certain you have observed this sign in some form or another.

Hollywood Celebrities posing with their one eye symbolism.

It is also referred to as your Third Eye. But at its core, it represents only one thing: Lucifer. The Eye of Providence or the Eye of Lucifer.

Eye of Horus

It was supposed to represent God who watches over mankind.

It is not the God of the Bible. One eye has been a powerful symbol, having its roots in ancient Egyptian mythos. Also known as the Eye of Horus.

Eye of Horus on Egyptian caskets

The eye of Horus is often believed as the Egyptian sun god Horus, having an omnipresent vision over mankind.

It also represents secret or occult wisdom. It was used to be painted on Egyptian caskets because they hoped that it would help the dead soul to see its way through the afterlife. The eye is often associated with light and spirit.

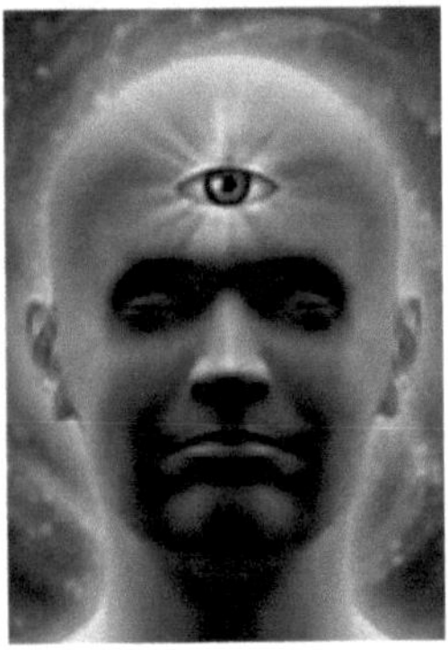

The third eye signified the higher self or higher consciousness. Our primary two eyes are for normal vision, but the third eye is the eye of wisdom. That is why many try to open their 3rd eye via yoga and meditation.

Can you see the similarities in these concepts?

It is just not the celebrities who make these one eye symbolism; all production houses release their movies with this symbol as their movie poster.

I have only collected a few out of many movie posters to show you this collage. I have not edited any of the posters here. You can search for them on the internet and see it for yourself. They all cannot be coincidences, right.

One eye Symbolism in Movie posters

Fashion Magazines depicting the one eye symbolism on their covers

I was perplexed when I discovered and compared these covers after covers. It is so common now to see that. Even the posters and images of big movies are doing it. They all have this one pose to make. Should I believe there are less creative people in the movie industry? Certainly not.

You probably wouldn't have noticed it if I hadn't placed them side by side. This is the level of subliminal messaging our generation is going through.

Katy Perry in a music video showing eye of horus

This is the same wisdom that was offered by the serpent to Adam and Eve before they ate the fruit. ***The spiritual knowledge of knowing Good and Evil.*** This wisdom tells you that Satan is the god of this world, and he rewards those who serve and worship him.

Have any of these images shocked you yet?

There is even more to come, with more pieces of evidence to support what I am saying. They are all hiding in plain sight. Next is:

Devil's Horns

This symbol is full of deception because over time it has represented many different things. The biggest deception is that this hand sign has been adapted for Rock n Roll.

Many youths believe this hand sign represents hard rock and rock music in general. That is a lie.

This is how this sign has been made popular among teens and music enthusiasts. It also got more famous among children because Spiderman makes this same hand sign when he shoots his webs.

I too plead guilty of making this hand sign out of coolness and ignorance during my school and college days; that is why I do not hold anyone accountable for the same.

In reality, this hand sign is used to cast curse spells by Satanists. According to Anton LaVey: the founder of the Church of Satan, the index finger, and the little finger work in spreading their curses. Wider the fingers are made, wider the curse gets projected. Similar to how a shotgun would work.

He said this on a live Joe Pyne T.V show in 1967, from which I have shown this picture below.

I have also searched the internet and have created yet another collage of instances where these celebrities are making the devil's horns in public. You can spot celebrities from all fields here.

Devil's horns made by various celebrities

This curse symbol, also known as the Devil's Horns, is often flashed in commercials and music videos.

Let us study an example. There is an Indian soft drink ad that uses this hand symbol to promote a certain soda refreshment company. Here, the meaning of the devil's horns has completely been changed to represent something stylish and cool.

The main aim of darkness is to bombard your subconscious with all these symbols so much that you start admiring these things in your life and soon adopt them too.

That is why so many young individuals casually make the devil's horns without knowing what it really means. Ask my friends, I was also guilty of the same.

That is why you will see similar ads like this one at every turn of the street. ***The more the message is repeated, the faster your subconscious mind will adapt to it.*** After a certain point in time, you will get desensitized to its presence. Because of such desensitization, you will be more tolerant of their evils till the arrival of the Antichrist.

The evidence is all around us. If you have made any of these hand signs and think it represents something else. You are deceived. This might not look like a big deal to you at the moment, but I request you to just think of all the incidents which were once labeled as conspiracy theories, but they actually came to be true. We often overlook them because they are not inconvenient to us yet. But I fear that the future is near when we have to make a conscious decision whether to join them or to be against them.

If we become too comfortable in their existence, it would be relatively harder for us to go against them when the time comes where brute force will be used over the ones who do not comply with their agenda.

Have no tolerance for these hand signs. Identify them now that you are aware.

Are these pieces of information too much? We have a few more hand signs to discuss. I want you to re-read everything that we have covered so far. These things are hard to process but are necessary in the times we are living in.

Darkness always presents their agenda disguised as cool, and stylish, often targeting the younger generation.

"Here is wisdom. Let him who has understanding calculate the number of the beast, for it is the number of a man: his number is **666**."

Revelation 13:18

The 666 hand sign

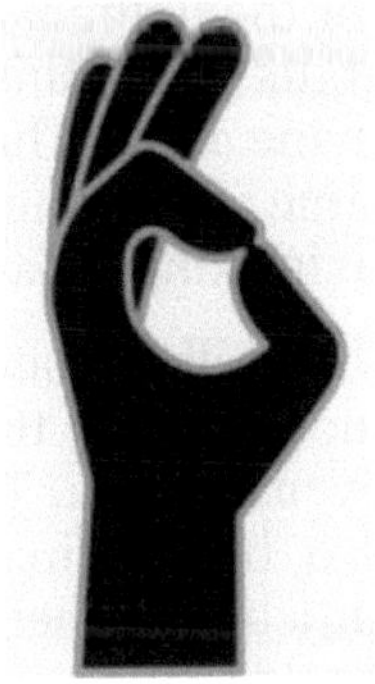

This is the most deceiving symbol out of them all. This symbol communicates so many different things and is used by people to represent so many different ways. Any of the things the masses use to describe this sign isn't true at all.

A decade ago, this sign was meant to show "Okay" or "OK". But now, rarely do people use it to display that. Now they are used for various other representations. For the NBA, it means a 3-pointer. Referees in the NFL, use it for 3rd down and in other sports where the number 3 is represented.

Celebrities, singers and pop stars flash this sign and they don't even tell us what it means. It is so weird to see people putting their hands on their eyes and making the OK sign. Why do they do that? What is the meaning of making a 666 hand sign over their one eye and posing for a photo-shoot?

And lastly, it is a hand gesture or mudra used for yoga and meditation. The reason is to finally open their 3rd eye. Can you connect the dots now?

Opening the 3rd eye is to raise your consciousness and communicate with a familiar spirit from the 2nd heavens. Everything is connected.

For the illuminated ones, it means something different. At its core, this symbol means the approval of the divine king. Their coming lord of light (used in the game of thrones): Lucifer - the Light Bearer. Their divine king is Satan himself.

These illuminated ones are the ones who have the knowledge of the good and evil which their lord has given to them. They are known as the Illuminati. They also believe in a Messiah, but that Messiah is the Antichrist. Their Messiah will bring about the New World Order.

I have prepared a collage of pictures where many worldwide celebrities are making the 666 hand sign in the form of OK over their one eye.

"A-Ok" Sign Satanic Meaning
ILLuminati Eye of Lucifer
666
ILLUMINATI Symbolism
Number of the AntiChrist Beast
666 + One Eye handsign by all popular celebrities you may know

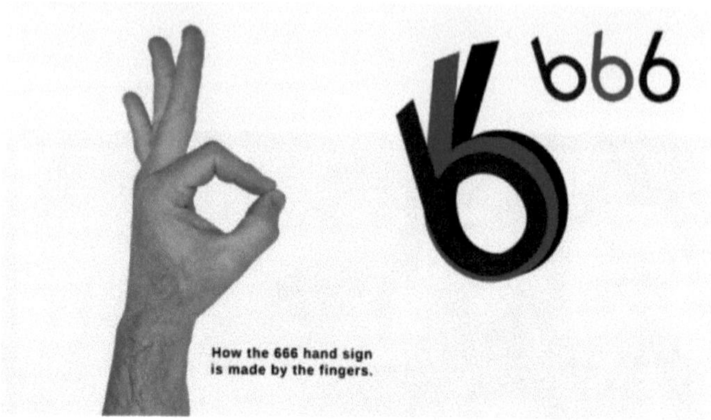

It is believed that 90% of our favorite actors and actresses, singers and rappers, athletes, politicians are some way or the other connected with them, or else they won't be having their celebrity podium. Humans of all ages are conditioned that these signs are harmless. Even kids cartoons are not spared from this. They are being used as their agenda platform, too.

This came as a big shocker to me when I was in my research. A lot of celebrities whom I had admired in the past had their allegiance to Satan and his kingdom of darkness. That was the truth. Just not celebrities, but big corporations are involved in these symbolisms too. You can identify them by their logos.

Do not get desensitized of their presence.

Here are a few of many global company logos that are designed having all the above hand signs that we have discussed. You can easily notice the one eye and the 666 symbolisms now.

Examples of few Corporations having the combination of these symbols in their logos

How will I know who is a sellout and who is deceived?

Good question. Just because you see someone making these hand symbols does not mean they are sellouts. They are either ignorant or deceived into believing otherwise. Many throwing these signs are just confused and don't have enough knowledge of what they are making. They mainly do it because they see their favorite celebrity or music diva or politician throw that sign, so they just copy them. Because they idolize them. Even I stand guilty of the same. In my ignorant college days, I used to make devil's horn signs almost every time I posed for a picture. Was I evil and was I supporting them and their agenda? **No.**

But trust me, there are many who are public figures and are sell-outs. They purposefully throw these hand signs to deceive you. The way you know the difference is by reviewing them completely and just not judging them by only one picture.

The ones who have sold their souls to the devil will try to throw these symbols all the time. If any individual is idolized by many, and has a big platform of influence, if then they make these symbols: in their photo-shoots, in their music videos, during their live performances, making similar tattoos all over their bodies, highlighting these symbols, etc...Those are the ones who are sellouts.

You will know them by the fruits they bear.

"Even so, every good tree bears good fruit, but a bad tree bears bad fruit. A good tree cannot bring forth evil fruit, neither can a corrupt tree bring forth good fruit."

Matthew 7: 17-18

Inverted Cross

This was the last major symbol I covered in my research. This is a sinister symbol that is used to represent Satan the most (in Hollywood horror movies).

Apostle Peter was crucified on an inverted cross by the Romans because he considered it unworthy to be crucified as his Lord Jesus. The inverted cross was a symbol of unworthiness and humility that was used during that time.

I have observed that it is used as a mockery of the Messiah and His church. A symbol of destroying the body of Christ, because, according to Matthew 16:18, Peter is the rock on which Jesus' church is built.

Even the throne of the Catholic pope has this symbol engraved. At this level of power, it is not a mistake, is it. They are certainly giving a subliminal message to us of who is the actual god of the pope.

The sad thing is how Catholics draw the sign of the cross over their heads and shoulders. If you only observe properly, you will notice that our Catholic brothers and sisters draw the inverted cross sign on their bodies instead of the straight cross.

However, their intentions are definitely noble, but this is the wrong way of making the cross. It should not be inverted. You are indirectly insulting Jesus by drawing the inverted cross. Check the hand movement stages from 1 to 4 in this diagram.

You will clearly spot the error.

If you were making this hand movement to make the sign of the cross, you were wrong. Observe and rectify your gesture.

Catholics argue that this is the cross for Saint Peter, and that by making this cross, we acknowledge his sacrifice. But as per my study so far, ***Saint Peter was never meant to be worshiped***. The same goes for mother Mary as well. Saint Peter was one of the major disciples of Jesus who was called out by Him to be fishers of men (Read Luke 5:8-10).

Like mother Mary, Peter was also a sinful human being who needed grace & salvation, no different than you and me. Jesus deliberately picked sinners and tax collectors so that they could not boast on their own achievements, but only could glorify God for all they did as His chosen saints.

One thing I started observing among religious Christians and Catholics was that they did a lot of idol worshiping. Huge idols of crucified Jesus, mother Mary, St. Peter, idols of archangels etc... No different than other idols worshiping religions that I am familiar with. As per what I was learning, Jesus didn't command to worship lifeless idols; instead, one should fall in humility and genuinely repent for their sins and ask God for forgiveness.

Also, regarding idol worship, the cross where Jesus is shown crucified signifies that Jesus is worshiped in His crucified/tortured state, i.e. His death on the cross is the last stand. But that is not the end, actually. **Jesus is Risen**. You should worship the risen Lord Jesus who has defeated & conquered death. Not when He was suffering for our sins.

My intention is to only tell you what I was observing and learning from my on-going research at that moment. We are all made in the image of God.

We all have our free will to follow or not to follow anything. Do not worry, but repent to our savior, and you will be forgiven. After all, He knows our hearts and intentions behind all our acts.

"Now the works of the flesh are evident, which are: adultery, fornication, uncleanness, lewdness, idolatry, sorcery, hatred, contentions, jealousies, outbursts of wrath, selfish ambitions, dissensions, heresies, envy, murders, drunkenness, revelries, and the like; of which I tell you beforehand, just as I also told you in time past, that those who practice such things will not inherit the kingdom of God."

Galatians 5:19-21

Wicca or Witchcraft

Before talking about this, I will give you just enough information to make you aware of them and identify their presence in our culture. I am no expert on this, but have kept a keen observation of things around me. It has entered our heads so quietly that you will be amazed at how it happened. Generally, there are 2 types of witchcraft.

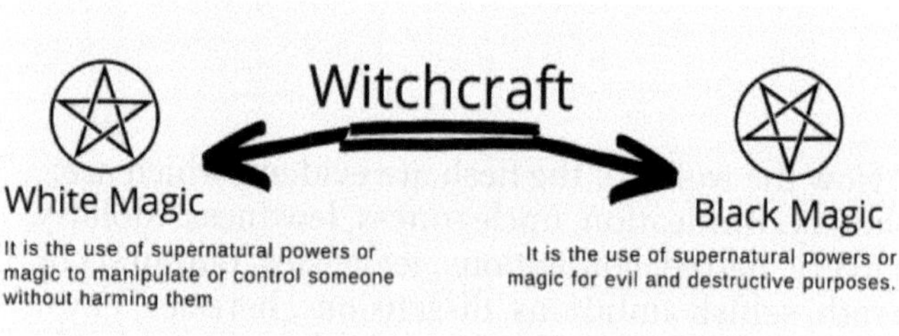

Just a reminder that white magic may look very kind, virtuous, and noble on a surface level, but it is still evil. Witchcraft: white or black, are evil. Both are directed to manipulate you, to get the work done from you by the individual doing the witchcraft.

Witchcraft starts with manipulation, goes then to domination, and eventually has full possession.

Witches/Warlocks are motivated by their own selfish desires and they achieve these by various spells and ungodly rituals. Often they wear jewelry of an inverted cross, representing a mockery of Jesus' sacrifice. They use tarot cards and divination to predict the future supernaturally.

Many innocent people, who are not saved, constantly worry about their future and thus visit such fortune tellers. ***Do not be a partake r in any of these*.**

The end result is always destructive to your soul. They open many doors to the supernatural, and the spirits that enter through those doors want to harm you. They enter to steal, kill and destroy your peace and lives. The worst part is that you will not know that until it is too late.

White magic, out of the two is the most deceiving one out there because it disguises itself to be harmless, cool, virtuous and modern. As if it is a trend now to become a witch.

This is the very same thing that I saw in the fifth Harry Potter movie back in my teenage years. As earlier explained, it captivated my mind because I saw the white magic practitioners fighting the black magic practitioners. Since God was guiding me in it, I was not influenced much by them.

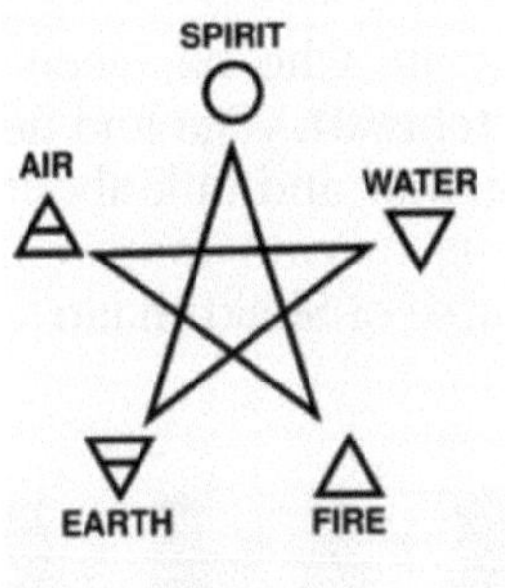

The best way to identify white magic: by the five elements that form it. These 5 elements in the diagram come together to bind a spell.

Does that ring a bell from anywhere? From some of your childhood shows maybe. Let me give you some examples.

There were many shows that we as children used to enjoy, which had concepts of witchcraft and dabbling with unclean spirits in it. And we used to love watching these beloved shows.

The first example would be a show from Cartoon Network. A series called the Captain Planet, where there are 5 planeteers who have "magical" rings of earth, wind, fire, water, and heart/spirit which combine together and summon Captain Planet.

I hope you remember watching this cartoon show.

The second example on my list will be India's first-ever superhero: Shaktimaan. One of the most anticipated shows in India during the 1990s.

The entire origin of this superhero character is based upon unlocking the inner powers via waking up the kundalini and 7 chakras via yoga and gaining all the 5 elemental powers of wind, earth, fire, water, and spirit.

Anyone who has seen the episodes can remember it. Witchcraft, yoga and new age philosophy often tie close together and talk about attaining higher consciousness so as to gain more enlightenment and was the main source of Shaktimaan's power.

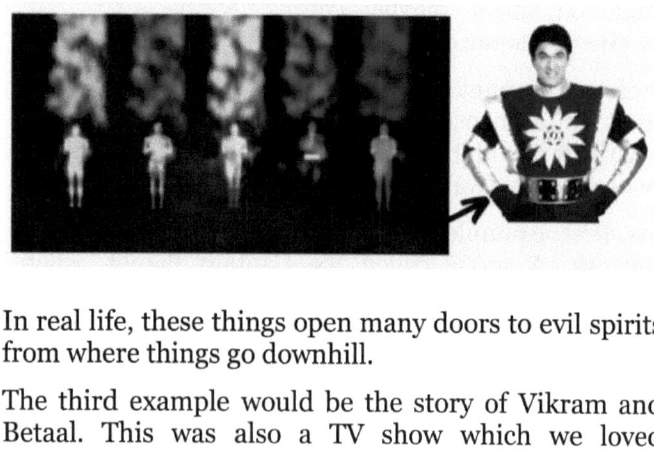

In real life, these things open many doors to evil spirits from where things go downhill.

The third example would be the story of Vikram and Betaal. This was also a TV show which we loved watching during the 1990s. It is a mythological story of a King named Vikramaditya, where he was tasked to carry a corpse which hung from a tree. The individual who gave this task was seeking some occult powers, which he would get only and only if a king like Vikram brought it to him. Meanwhile, during the journey, the spirit of Betaal used to narrate a story to Vikram, and after completing the story, he would ask a witty question.

During the narration, if the King broke silence, the spirit would fly off and hang from that tree. Thus the entire carrying process was to be repeated.

If the King knew the answer, he was bound to respond; otherwise Betaal would crack his head into pieces. But if he does speak out, the King would break the vow of silence, and Betaal would fly back to the treetop, leaving the king inches short of his destination. The king would go after the demon and start all over again.

This is a repetitive loop pattern of new short-stories that Betaal narrates to the king and he fetches him back. This story wants you to focus on that only. So that you don't put much thought into the core of its existence, which was in the occult.

Now that I analyze it, this show was highly demonic, focuses on occult practices, and on a witty demonic spirit called Betaal. As an innocent child, I never felt it weird but just saw it as entertainment. Concepts like these should not be targeted towards innocent children.

So many of my childhood shows have been exposed in my phase 1 research that I cannot list them all.

Personally, I was sad and was almost in a state of denial that these things were not true at all. There can be a better explanation to all these.

But as I kept digging up on this topic, I became certain. Accepting and embracing witchcraft and demonic spirits was the subliminal message in these shows and was fed to us right, left and center.

The Concept of granting 3 wishes

Just like the 5 elements, in white magic or white witchcraft, there is a concept to create spells that grant you 3 wishes. No more, no less. And this is perfectly reflected in the many cartoon shows and anime we have watched over the years.

For Example:

The first example is of a Disney cartoon series called Aladdin, where he gets a magic lamp with a genie in it.

The genie grants 3 wishes to Aladdin, which he fulfills as commanded. Generally, genies or gins are not considered friends in any culture. Mainly it is believed to be an evil spirit who is captured in a lamp, and anyone who owns the lamp is the master of that spirit inside the lamp.

Now that spirit is responsible for fulfilling any 3 wishes that the master has for him. Showing that gins can be like friends provides a misconception among young minds who consume such cartoon shows every day.

Personally, I have fantasized as a kid to have a personal genie who would fulfill all my wishes. These wrong portrayals definitely bend reality a little bit in every kid's mind, which is dangerous according to me.

The second example is a Japanese anime television series called Dragon Ball Z, where a dragon used to be summoned by collecting 7 dragon balls which would fulfill 3 wishes. The most common wish the characters of that anime had was to bring people back from the dead. Sort of a resurrection, so to speak.

I realized that these shows are mocking Jesus as He died and rose from the dead.

They subconsciously make you believe that anyone can die and come back alive, just by summoning the dragon. They even have a character called Mr Satan on the show. How obvious can it be?

With all these shows as evidence, here is a collection of all the symbolism I noticed in children's cartoon shows. They are taken from all kids' shows. I have included some comic book pictures as well here.

Movies on Witchcraft

The most effective way our generation is desensitized to witchcraft is through Hollywood movies. There are many movies like Dr. Strange, Oz, or Maleficent, but the biggest one in my opinion is the Harry Potter movie series.

This movie series is actually based on actual novels of the same name. The writer of this novel: J.K. Rowling, first had the idea for the story while delayed on a train traveling from Manchester to London's King's Cross during the 1990s. This series has targeted the millennial generation for a decade and has presented witchcraft and wizardry in a very cool & stylish way, bringing many original occult spells in front of kids without anyone suspecting them as what they are. BEWARE.

I am a millennial myself and have witnessed this since 2001 where kids were crazy for these Harry Potter movies. This is what a Reverend has to say about the Harry Potter books:

> *"The curses and spells used in the books are actual curses and spells; which when read by a human being risk conjuring evil spirits into the presence of the person reading the text."*
>
> *Reverend Daniel J. Reehil*

These types of horror/occult movies encourage innocent kids to play with Ouija boards, Charlie-Charlie, Bloody Mary, witch game, voodoo, etc..etc.. all because they were curious and saw a movie depicting it on the big screen. Kids try out these spells that are shown in these movies and TV shows as if that is something heroic and cool. But what they don't know is that it will eventually harm their souls in the long run.

They ENTER your life through ENTER-TAINMENT.

If that was not so, then an occultic day like Halloween would have not got any recognition among common people. They are now celebrated fondly without a question, by people who would have banned it if they knew what long term harm they do. Ask the question why do we need to celebrate demonic holidays?

It is the duty of every born again Christian to make the common people understand these truths. And even these movies, music and entertainment demonstrate what eventually happens to people who go deep into witchcraft and the occult. They don't hide the facts and the side effects it has, but still the enchantment of the spells are so high that kids or teenagers ignore the bad stuff and adopt these witchcraft practices anyways.

Another concern of mine is when people buy healing crystals, tarot cards, spell books and new-age self-help books that guide people step by step into increasing their conscious levels, tuning in with the universe as if it's a living/breathing thing, connecting to dead relatives and channeling positive affirmations by playing high frequency sounds waves.

These practices open up portals to familiar spirits and are a form of practicing witchcraft. These familiar spirits are demons.

DO NOT BUY OR PRACTICE THEM.

I have seen few testimonial videos of ex-witches and ex-satanists who have come out of these dark places and have warned us through their testimonies of what horrors lie if you continue deep into witchcraft and the occult.

I would highly recommend you to read the book: Out of the Devil's Cauldron by John Ramirez.

An ex-satanist who overcame the kingdom of darkness and entered into the kingdom of light. It was very informative in my research and has exposed the kingdom of darkness far better than I ever could.

Another brother in Christ has perfectly defined what witchcraft truly is, and he has permitted me to use his findings to share with you in this book. Read it below and be aware of the evil.

What is Witchcraft?

Witchcraft can be defined as the performance of magic forbidden by God for non-biblical ends. The word witchcraft is related to the old English word Wiccan, i.e. "practice of magical arts."

When a person becomes a witch, he or she enters into a pact with Satan to worship him. They deny the Creator of heaven and earth. They deny their baptism with Christ. They deny the worship formerly paid to God. They adhere to the devil and believe only in him. They are re-baptized in the devil's name. They request of the devil for their names to be written in the Book of Death. They tattoo themselves with the devil's mark on various parts of their body. The mark might vary in shape - magic circle or number 666; serpent, evil eye, spider, bat, a rabbit foot, a toad, etc.

Witches were supposed to have had a variety of different powers that kept the people in fear of them. Witchcraft practitioners place spells by some spoken word(s) or form of words believed to have magic powers, binding them by spell or charm. In witchcraft there is white magic, which is supposedly curative and black magic, also voodoo (African name it joojoo) which is destructive.

BIBLICAL CONDEMNATION OF WITCHCRAFT

By: Brother Mathew Sammie

Lastly, there is one specific movie that I wanted to cover. It is a regional (Bengali) movie of East India but is worth every bit of mentioning here. The movie is called *Goopy Gyne Bagha Byne,* which was released back in 1969.

The story is about Goopy and Bagha, who were banished from their kingdom for being bad musicians. However, with their skills, they succeed in pleasing the king of the ghosts (Bhooter Raja) who grants them three wishes.

Who is the king of ghosts in this movie? Who else can that be other than Satan himself? Now today in real life, with what will you compare this story plot with?

Illustration art depicting the meeting scene with Bhooter Raja

It sounds similar to an aspiring singer/actor today, who wants to earn fame and money in the music industry, sells his or her soul to the devil, and their wishes are fulfilled for signing record albums, fame and money.

This was the movie I have watched countless times on cable TV with my family since I was growing up and didn't know what I was consuming. But the wisdom of God revealed this to me. The fruits of evil are always a curse.

I started noticing these once I was aware of their existence in plain sight. The subliminal messaging has been bombarded on us since 1969. Wake up folks if you are still asleep.

A change in me that I observed was that now these signs and symbols were not affecting my subconscious mind anymore.

Since I was researching them heavily, I was now able to identify them with my conscious mind every time I saw them. It was no more subliminal to me and I hope the same for you.

Do not take my words for it, do your own unbiased research, and find it out.

World's Evil

After studying and digging through all these things, I have developed a good understanding of why the world today is so lost with their moral standings. We now see a dramatic shift in our morals and values over time.

Over decades, we have seen these symbols, cartoons, and movies desensitizing us. And gradually, we are observing our moral fabric shifting and changing. More towards sin and evil.

Our society is shaped by our morals and beliefs. And these are affected by what we watch, read, see, and hear. What is acceptable in our society today was once completely non-acceptable, even 50 years ago. As a culture, we are shifting at a very high speed.

When people blatantly show the devil's horns sign out in public without properly knowing what they really meant, leads me to see the fruits of this carnal world on human minds. Would your grandfather in the 1950s & 60s have flashed devil's horns or 666 hand signs in public?

I think not.

So why is it so common today among youth? What is fueling this? This is a problem and needs proper addressing.

This is so because of what has subliminally been taught to us over time. Very subtle and consistent programming of our Subconscious. We have become more tolerant of evil now as compared to our older generation. As if our senses had been neutralized. Especially on topics like **Sex, Violence, Language, Blasphemy** etc...

Having sex before marriage is now the norm. Turning violent, depressed, and stressed for small issues is also common. Even people openly brag about them on social media platforms and make short videos about how depressed and alone they are. People now follow and worship Instagram influencers as if they were idols.

Using abusive language in our everyday vocabulary: Put a big tick on it. And finally blasphemy. Using God's name as a cuss word. Where should I even begin?

Will you ever take your mother's name as a cuss word out in the public? No? Why not? It is so because it will dishonor her name. But somehow taking the name of Jesus Christ while cursing is OK. The name of Jesus Christ is taken so often as a cuss word, even I used to say that before my research journey began. It should never be like that.

A lot of this is coming from what the mass media is presenting to us in the form of Music, Movies, Video games, Television, Sports, Social media, etc... They have thrown conservative values out of the window and have promoted evil practices as hip, cool and modern.

We have completely forgotten the values of our grandparents' generation in what we find appropriate in mass consumption.

Let me give a few examples.

These web series glorify satanism, witchcraft, and the occult, all in the name of looking cool, stylish and taking vengeance is a good thing. They are not even hiding it. Simply ask this question to yourself: Would your grandma allow you to consume this media if she were around?

The answer is: **NEVER.**

Your grandparents would have got a mild shock if they saw what modern web series shows in the name of entertainment. They would have canceled all your subscriptions and would have started praying for their grandchildren every waking second.

Because of what they show, the graphics and stories they portray, slowly morphs our ideology bit by bit according to what they are showing. They morph your mind so that you freely choose whatever they project. They are indirectly forcing you to their agenda and will by repeating this over and over again. Brilliant but evil.

When I started to dig a little deeper, so many more issues arose which were all connected to this dramatic shift in culture. I am referring to the various principalities that run the urban life we know.

The way government taxes are set, the way money works, the way we buy and sell. It was very different just a few decades ago. We used to grow our own food, had independent businesses, and going to church or temple was a community thing.

Everything is connected

In India, the 1990s and the 2020s look way different. And the world is running away from the true Jesus as fast as a thief who runs from the law-keepers. Ungodliness is rampant.

All of these things are connected. Since the gold standard was removed from the dollar bill by the U.S President Richard Nixon in 1971, the dollar currency was backed up by debt and not by gold. Debt became the new money of the 20th century instead of Gold.

You will work for your loans, mortgages, and credit score so that they profit from you. That is what debt does. How did they sell this to us?

Answer: The idiot box.

It's the modern-day slavery. Slavery was never abolished; it changed its form. The chart below shows how this carnal, sinful world is being run and who is in control. The elites, who want to control the entire world, want to challenge God and everything He loves.

They want to control the population of the world and finally bring about the New World Order, which will manipulate, control, and then dominate you under one global economy and under One Religion.

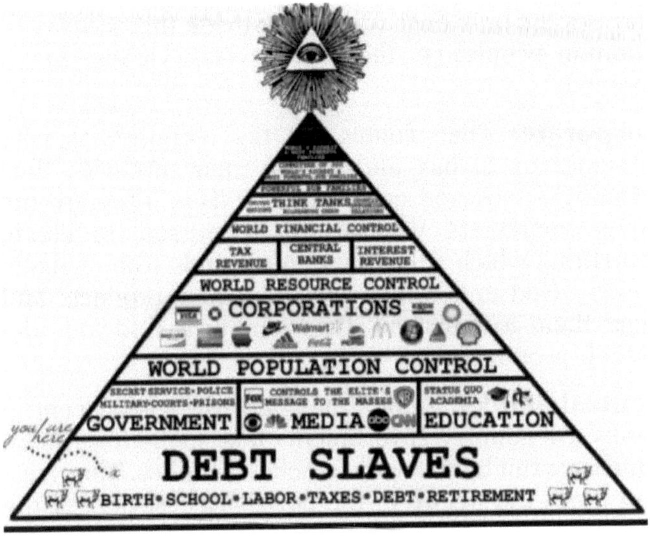

This is the chart that shows the hierarchy of who belongs where. It's a pyramid structure and there is always someone at the top pulling the strings on the ones below. The one on the top of the pyramid is the god of this world.

The Debt Slaves: We all fall under the bottom category. The ones who take loans, debt, and pay them off by taking 2 jobs or by doing overtime. We are considered slaves who work for money.

Government, Media, Education: Next comes the manipulating platform of the media, government, and education universities. Their work is to sell us a dream so that we follow that which keeps us in line. Or, to better put it, keeps us in fear.

They sold the idea that a college degree is a must for you to succeed in life. Get a well-paying, secured job and settle down and do not question the system much.

Over time, they have successfully managed to brainwash us that there is something called security in the form of free healthcare and free education, and that they are the only ones who will provide this security to common people, i.e. the bottom class. Or else life is doomed.

Corporate: Then comes the big corporations who influence us to buy and idolize their products, thus bringing a new god called *materialism*. They are the expert marketers who are in a pursuit to create something which will deviate our minds from actually seeking God and rather consume their products and make them gods instead. They want us to find your idol in their products or services.

Central Banks: Above them are the global central banks. All country governments take loans from them which are run by the world's richest families. They have 100 times the wealth of the Forbes richest man of the year. They are never shown on any magazine cover, nor are they interviewed. They are the ones who control all the classes below them.

The Pyramid Chief: And above them all, we see the final puppet master who controls the entire pyramid. The actions to be carried out and give instructions to the elite to make his will come true. It is Satan himself: the god of this world.

The Idiot Box

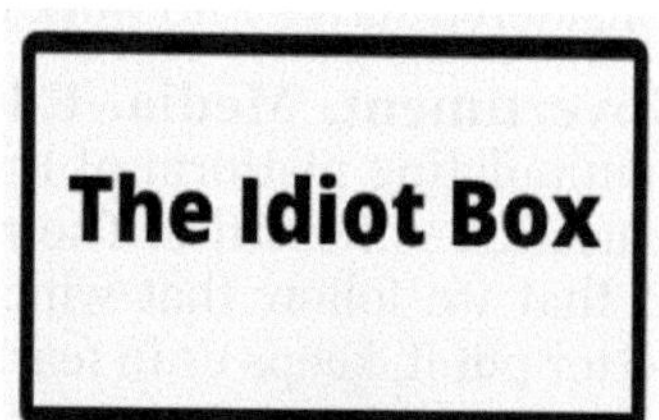

Television is seen as a great source of entertainment and enjoyment. But I see it as a great tool for mind control. It is a tool used by the elites to keep you chasing materialistic goods and being in a consumer or debt lifestyle.

Starting with TV shows to commercials, television has made your brain idle and focuses on materialistic pleasures over self-development. It is a tool now operational for many decades which is molding your and your kid's brains to the agenda of the NWO (new world order).

I have shown you many images as evidence by now to build my case. It is now that you understand when the news channels, talk shows, TV series, etc... Spread a certain idea and suppress/bans the counter-thoughts, they are molding your worldview in compliance with their agenda.

Fear and anger are what they spread through this idiot box to those who are constantly consuming it. As previously stated, they influence little kids with their agendas and occult practices to warp their brains. No wonder why little kids these days learn abusive languages so fast. Always remember:

They ENTER through ENTER-TAINMENT.

Also because of television, actors, and actresses are worshiped as gods. People go completely crazy to see them on TV, in theatres, and when they are live in person. If that is not mind control, what is?

My Tipping point

The New Year 2017 came. In my quest for finding the truth so far, I have dug into the darkness we live in. By now, I know the mess this world is in and needs a serious do-over. Something to pause and reset this entire world to become livable.

Though all the things this fallen world has done and is doing in plain sight, it did not tip me off into accepting Jesus in my life yet. I was not even thinking about it. I knew all the satanic symbolism, gestures and everything the darkness had in their belt was pure evil, but what could I do in all of this?

One thing that I constantly observed was that mocking Jesus was very fashionable among these celebrities. This kept bugging me greatly, why is Jesus only targeted by these evil elites? Why not Krishna or Buddha or Guru Nanak? Why not Allah? They all are celebrated and are considered very inclusive. If you are so inclusive, then why leave Jesus behind?

Even drawing a picture of Muhammad becomes a great offense to the Muslim community. Why is no one taking any offense when Jesus is being mocked? Just not mocked but humiliated. Making a cuss word out of His name is too much dishonour.

I have never heard Allah's name being used as a cuss word. Have you? No. You will be instantly labelled as an islamophobe and will be ridiculed by the satanic mainstream media. I have never heard the term christianophobie or anyone ever held accountable for insulting Jesus.

Do people find pleasure in mocking Jesus? Why Jesus only?

My phase 1 research was very successful and made a perfect foundation for the direction to go in. Thus the Phase 2 research began as I started digging deeper into why Jesus is only mocked?

FOR

God

SO **LOVED** THE WORLD

THAT HE GAVE HIS ONLY **SON**

THAT WHOEVER **BELIEVES** IN HIM

SHALL NOT PERISH BUT HAVE

EVERLASTING LIFE.

JOHN 3:16

Phase 2 Research

What has Jesus done?

This was the 2nd Phase of my research. The series of dominos were falling right into their places. By now I have good knowledge of all that I have shared and know who the evil one is. The 1st Phase was completed. I roughly knew the story of Adam and Eve. But had no idea of what it represented.

I now started to see what the deal with Jesus was, and this is what I came to know.

Jesus was a Jew from a small and unpopular town of Nazareth, Israel, who claimed to be the Son of God. To back it up, He did various miracles, prophecies, and eventually sacrificed His life as a ransom to pay the debt of all our sins. That whoever believes in Him shall not die but have eternal life. - John 3:16

He was supposed to be the king and the Messiah who would defeat the Roman Empire and free Israel from taxation and oppression. But Jesus claimed to free us from our sins and spiritual death instead. He was not at all interested in setting up an earthly kingdom, but a sort of kingdom, which was not of this world. - John 18:36.

"My kingdom is not of this world. If My kingdom were of this world, My servants would fight, so that I should not be delivered to the Jews; but now My kingdom is not from here."

John 18:36

But the Jews wanted a strong King who would wage war on Rome and free them. Unfortunately, Jesus was not fitting that caricature of the Messiah they wanted. So He was handed to Rome for the crime of blasphemy, to give Him the most shameful and horrifying punishment; i.e. the Roman crucifixion.

Jesus was not only crucified but got 39 Roman scourges too. The usual torture equipment was a short whip with several (approx. 9) single or braided leather thongs of variable lengths.

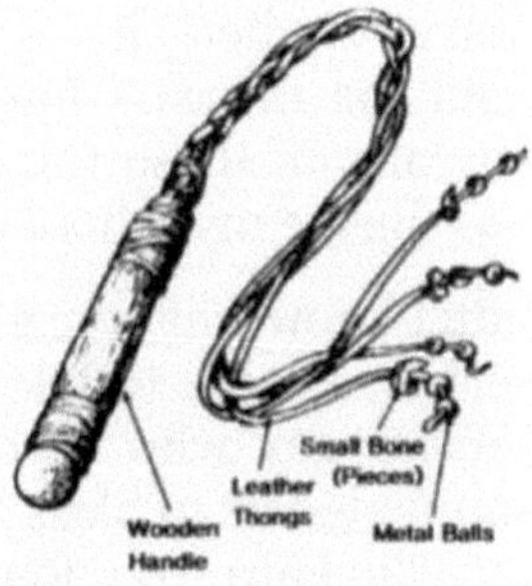

Sharp, rugged bones, broken glass, iron balls with sharp grooves were attached to these leather thongs so that it would be easy to stick to the victim's flesh and tear it up.

These bad boys were designed to bring immense pain on the victim. After the scourges, Jesus' flesh was hanging from His body like ribbons, and anyone hardly recognized Him.

On top of that, He had to carry His own cross on His back to the Mount of Golgotha, where He was painfully crucified outside Jerusalem alongside two criminals.

To better understand this, watch the movie: **The Passion of the Christ by Mel Gibson**. The above pictures are taken from that movie itself. This movie has shown Jesus' last 12 hours before the crucifixion in the most historically accurate way possible.

But was that the end? **No**. As Jesus had claimed before, He rose from the dead on the 3rd day. Jesus has defeated death.

I have studied in a convent school for 12 years but I didn't know any of these things about Jesus during my school time.

I didn't know what the gospel even was or meant. In my research, I came to know that Jesus was a completely harmless guy who tried to do good for all. He even commanded us to bless your enemies and to do good to them who harm you. Read Matthew 5:44

Till now I was looking into things in a very superficial way, and so the solution to anything was a little blur. Till now, only my brain was with me. To better understand the solution, I have to include my heart as well, along with my brain.

"But I say to you, love your enemies, bless those who curse you, do good to those who hate you, and pray for those who spitefully use you and persecute you."

Matthew 5:44

Scrutiny

Now, I was not looking at Jesus for research purposes, but in a much personal way. I knew that just standing like an umpire and looking over the facts would lead me no-where. The brute torture done on Jesus was completely unjustified, especially for someone, who came to do so much for us. It just made no sense.

Many, and I really mean many have claimed to be God across time and regions, but no one has done anything worthy to back up their claim. If Jesus really rose from the dead, that would really make Him divine. Something solid to back up His claim. So I asked these 3 questions for verification.

1. Can Jesus be historically verified?
2. Did Jesus really rise from the dead?
3. Does the message of the Bible get corrupted over time?

For these 3 answers especially, I have to judge everything with a rational mind and not with emotions. Evidence with proper historical data has to be my lead for the investigation. Because now it was different. It was personal. These are the answers that I got.

Question 1: Can Jesus be historically verified?

Jesus was one of the easiest people to research because of the way dating years are numbered. B.C. means "*Before Christ*" and B.C.E. stands for "*Before the Common Era*". They are the same. And A.D. means Anno Domini - Latin for "*in the year of the Lord*" referring to the birth of Jesus Christ. C.E., the abbreviation for "*Common Era*" is used to mark time in the same way.

The entire dating system goes along with the birth of Jesus. Jesus literally splits time into 2 parts. It is 2021 (when this book is written) i.e. Jesus's age would be 2021 years.

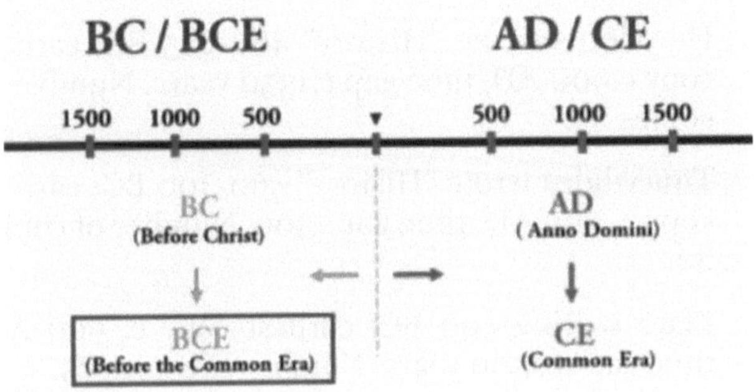

Jesus of Nazareth was crucified in Jerusalem under the orders of Pontius Pilate, the Governor of the Roman province of Judaea, around 30-33 A.D. This is a historical fact.

The Roman Government had excellent documentation for the ones they crucified. It is purely laughable when many claim that Jesus has never existed or is a mythological character. These are the same people who believe Santa Claus is real.

The Quran is the only historically claimed document that denies Jesus was crucified. But it cannot be legit, as it first originated in 632 A.D. Almost 600 years after the actual incident, the book was also written by only man and not by eyewitnesses to the event.

The Greek historians, Roman historians, Pagan historians, Jewish historians, and Christian historians see the earliest data as evidence instead. I also looked for the earliest historical data on the matter. The closer the record data at the time of the crucifixion, the better.

Next, you will see a list. These are the people who give us the ancient history of the world, and they are studied at the graduate level and are not at all disputed as myth or fiction.

- Homer wrote "Iliad" 800 BC; earliest copy from c.400 BC; time gap c.400 years. Number of copies 6432.
- Herodotus wrote "History" 480-425 BC; earliest copy c.900 AD, time gap c.1350 years. Number of copies 83.
- Thucydides wrote "History" 460-400 BC; earliest copy c. 900 AD; time gap 1300. Number of copies 84.
- Plato writing 400 BC; earliest copy c. 900 AD, time gap c. 1300 years. Number of copies 75.
- Caesar wrote "Gallic Wars" 100-44 BC; earliest copy c. 900 AD; time gap 1000 years. Number of copies 106.
- Tacitus wrote "Annals" AD 100; earliest copy c. 1100; time gap c. 1000 years. Number of copies 207.
- Pliny Secundus wrote "Natural History" AD 61-113; earliest copy c. 850. Time gap 750, Number of copies 7.

Josh McDowell stated this in his book: *Evidence that Demands a Verdict*. This is the title; Josh wanted to write his book as an atheist, the evidence for disproving Christianity and debunking the resurrection of Jesus but ended up writing it to defend the Lord's resurrection and the Bible.

I would highly recommend this book to you.

There are good records of 1st-century Historians mentioning Jesus in their writings. You have to deny all of history in order to deny the existence of Jesus. The answer to the 1st question was blatantly clear.

Major non-Biblical History records on Jesus

This is a common question among many skeptics, where they ask for records from non-biblical sources which confirm the existence of Jesus.

I came to know some of the most prominent non-Christian figures from 1st century Israel, who gave an account of Jesus, and early Christians, existing during their lives.

1. Flavius Josephus (A.D. 37-100)

Flavius Josephus A.D. 37 - 100

Thought to have been born a few years after the crucifixion of Jesus around 37 A.D., The first-century Jewish historian Flavius Josephus was a well-connected aristocrat and military leader in Palestine who served as a commander in Galilee during the First Jewish Revolt against Rome between 66 and 70 A.D.

Although Josephus was not a follower of Jesus, he was around when the early church was getting started, so he knew people who had seen and heard Jesus.

He twice mentions Jesus in Jewish Antiquities, his massive 20-volume history of the Jewish people that was written around 93 A.D.

2. Cornelius Tacitus (A.D. 56-120)

Another account of Jesus appears in Annals of Imperial Rome, a first-century history of the Roman Empire written around 116 A.D. by the Roman senator and historian Cornelius Tacitus.

Cornelius Tacitus A.D. 56 - 120

In chronicling the burning of Rome in 64 A.D., Tacitus mentions that Emperor Nero falsely blamed the persons commonly called Christians, who were hated for their enormities. Christus, the founder of the name, was put to death by Pontius Pilate, procurator of Judea, in the reign of Tiberius.

3. Pliny the Younger (A.D. 62-113)

Shortly before Tacitus penned his account of Jesus, Roman governor Pliny the Younger wrote to Emperor Trajan that early Christians would "sing hymns to Christ as to a God."

Pliny the Younger A.D. 62 - 113

Q2. Did Jesus really rise from the dead as He claimed?

It hardly matters if Jesus was in history or not, if His claim of rising from the dead was not true. To better frame this question: **Is the Resurrection of Jesus true?**

If Jesus actually rose from the dead, His claim of being the only Son of God carries significant weight. On the other hand, if the resurrection never actually happened, then Jesus can be kept with all the other great historical characters that had a tragic death. The entire credibility of the Christian faith hangs on whether Jesus rose on the 3rd day or not?

"From that time forth began Jesus to show unto his disciples, how he must go unto Jerusalem, and suffer many things of the elders and chief priests and scribes, and be killed, and be raised again the third day."

Matthew 16:21

What are the historical facts that require explanation? And which explanations best account for these facts. These 3 facts are needed to be verified.

Fact 1: The Discovery of Jesus' Empty Tomb

Fact 2: The Appearances of risen Jesus after His death

Fact 3: The Disciples believed that Jesus rose from the dead and died horrible deaths professing it.

Fact 1:

Jesus rising from the dead is mentioned by six independent writers in the Bible. And some of these are the earliest materials to be found in the New Testament.

This is important because when an event is recorded by 2 or more unconnected sources, the confidence among historians that the event actually happened increases. The earlier these sources are dated, the higher their confidence.

Moreover, it was a woman who discovered that Jesus's body was missing. It was historic because the testimony of a woman in that era was considered next to worthless. A fabricated story would have replaced the woman with a man discovering Jesus' body.

Our confidence is further boosted by the response by the Jewish authorities. They blamed that Jesus's disciples would have removed the body, thereby admitting that the tomb was empty.

"Most scholars, by far, hold firmly to the reliability of the Biblical statements about the empty tomb."

Jacob Kremer, Professor of NT Studies, University of Vienna

Fact 2:

In one of the earliest letters of the New Testament, Paul provides a list of witnesses to Jesus' resurrection appearances. Jesus appeared to Peter, then to his 12 disciples, then to more than 500 people at one time, then to James, and finally to Paul. Read 1st Corinthians 15:5-8.

Also, Jesus met a man named Cleopas along with another disciple on the road to Emmaus after his resurrection. Read Luke 24:13–35.

However, they were not able to identify Jesus at the moment as they were travelling. They later came to know it was Jesus when Jesus broke bread with them.

A Greek Christian historian called Hegesippus (c. AD 180), who had composed his memoirs containing a varied mixture of historical, doctrinal, polemical, and catechetical interpolations. There, he mentioned that many years earlier, he had interviewed the grandsons of Jude the Apostle and learned that Clopas was the brother of Joseph: The husband of Mother Mary and the earthly father of Jesus.

This makes Luke 24: 13-35 historically accurate.

Fact 3:

After the death of Jesus, His disciples were devastated, horrified, and hid in fear for their lives. As Jews, they had no concept of a Messiah who would be executed by the enemies. Much less come back to life.

Moreover, in Jewish law, a punishment like the Roman crucifixion given to anyone like a criminal, meant that Jesus was literally under God's curse. Despite this belief, they sincerely came to know that Jesus was risen by God.

They were so completely convinced that even when threatened with death, not one of them recanted. Even a Pharisee named Saul who persecuted Christians suddenly became a Christian himself; so did Jesus' sceptical younger brother James.

This would have not been possible if it was not supernatural.

"Some sort of powerful transformative experience is required to generate the sort of movement the earliest Christianity was."

Luke Timothy Johnson. New Testament Scholar. Emory University.

Down through history, these historical facts were speculated to have various Naturalistic Explanations by sceptics. They were:

- The Conspiracy Theory
- Apparent Death Theory
- Displaced Body Theory and
- Hallucination Theory

The Conspiracy Theory

According to this theory, the disciples faked the resurrection. They stole Jesus' body from the tomb and lied that Jesus was alive, therefore creating the greatest hoax of all time.

However, this theory faced overwhelming objections. This theory was anachronistic as people of different time periods were judged by the moral standards of this era.

The 1st century Jews had no concept of a Messiah who was executed, and defeated by Israel's enemies, much less raised from the dead. In the Jewish faith, the resurrection was considered as a general event that happened after the end of the world which had no connection with the forthcoming Messiah.

The Conspiracy Theory also fails to explain the sincerity of the disciple's testimony. All of Jesus's disciples were brutally executed. No one does that if they are lying. They had nothing to gain financially by doing so. These people sincerely believed in the message they proclaimed and were willing to die violent deaths for it. Today, no scholar defends this conspiracy theory.

The Apparent Death Theory

This theory states that Jesus didn't really die on the cross. He revived inside the tomb, somehow escaped the Roman guards, and convinced His disciples that He rose from the dead.

This theory also has huge objections. It was not medically possible at all. The Romans were professional crucifixion killers. They checked each victim to see if they were dead before taking them down from the cross. Jesus somehow escaping the Romans in a tortured state was just not possible.

This theory is wildly implausible.

Hypothetically, even if Jesus was successful in fooling the Romans, and had a first-aid revival in the tomb, seeing a half-dead man coming out of a tomb who needed serious medical help would have a hard time convincing anybody of Jesus' glorious resurrection from the dead.

For all these reasons, no New Testament historian defends this theory.

Displaced Body Theory

This theory states that maybe Joseph of Arimathea placed Jesus' dead body in his tomb temporarily and then moved the body out, to the common graveyard. So, when the disciples came and saw the empty tomb, they concluded Jesus must have risen from the dead.

This theory fails because Jewish law, at that time strictly prohibited moving a corpse after it was interred except to the family tomb.

Also, the graveyard was geographically located close to where the crucifixion was done. Joseph would have informed the Romans that Jesus' dead body was moved by him while having the body as evidence buried in the grave for all to see.

No Jew in 1st century Israel wanted to be under the bad books of the Roman Empire. Any treason with them meant execution.

The Hallucination Theory

This is the last of the theories. It states that the disciples didn't see Jesus actually, but they imagined Jesus appeared to them. They were all hallucinating.

This theory faces one critical psychological issue. 1st, Jesus appeared not only one time, but many times in different locations, and to many people after He has risen. He even appeared to a group of more than 500 people at one time. Many unbelievers saw Him in His risen state too. There is nothing in any psychological case book that supports mass hallucinations. Hallucinations happen to only one individual, not to the masses.

As per Jewish law, a vision of anybody (hallucination) did not prove if the person was alive at that time, but the evidence that he was dead and had moved to the afterlife. Therefore, disproving the entire claim this theory wanted to prove.

This theory does not even explain the empty tomb. All these theories fail to explain the resurrection of Jesus. That means, it happened just as the disciples, who were the original eyewitnesses told us to be.

The 2nd question was nicely answered. Jesus defeated death and was raised in a glorified body.

Horrible Deaths of Jesus' Disciples

According to history, almost all of Jesus's disciples were killed in horrible ways, except for John. He died of old age. To escape this they could have easily lied that Jesus never rose from the dead, but they didn't. They gained no earthly fame, no money, no power to boast about, but still they never budged from their statement.

Andrew, Philip, Thaddeus, and Simon the Zealot were tortured and crucified like Jesus was.

Simon Peter refused to be crucified the same way as his Lord, so he was crucified on an upside-down cross, the symbol the kingdom of darkness uses extensively to mock Jesus.

James - son of Zebedee, was beheaded. Bartholomew was skinned alive. Thomas was speared to death. Matthew was stabbed to death. James - son of Alphaeus, was stoned to death.

These disciples preferred to die horrible deaths rather than denouncing Jesus and His resurrection. The price they paid to stand with the truth. Imagine that.

Question 3: Does the message of the Bible have been corrupted over time?

All of the above knowledge cannot be valid if the main source which we believe has been corrupted. Here is the answer that I got from this highly skeptic question.

Jesus spoke Aramaic in 1st century Israel. And the earliest 1st-century church used to speak Hebrew at that time. But by the time the New Testament was written to be added to the Septuagint Bible, it was done in the Greek language.

The chance of sustaining the core message of Jesus in a translation of a translation before it was ever written down was sceptical to me.

On top of it, the Latin Bible: Vulgate, which was published in 381 AD, lasted for more than a Millennium.

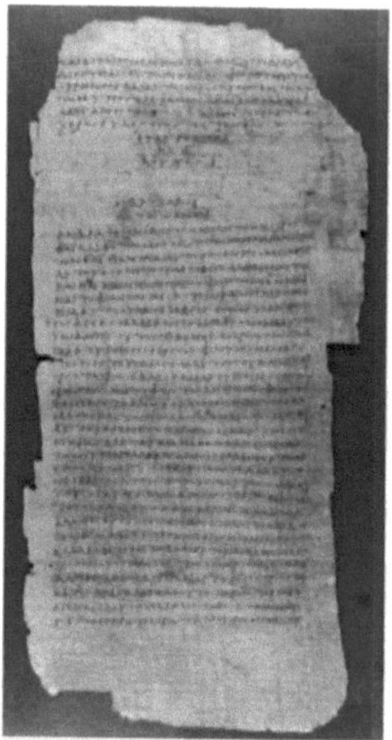

The earliest New Testament bible

Another translation from Greek to Latin before Martin Luther brought it into the German language during the 1500s. It was mass printed thanks to the invention of the Gutenberg printer. And then from the German language, it was finally translated to the English language in 1611 by King James, available even today as the King James Version (KJV).

How can the message of the New Testament Bible not get corrupted over translations? The answer is:

Jesus' apostles at that time were mostly multilingual since they were under Roman rule and used to travel to different places to spread the good news of Jesus Christ.

As their job demanded, they were experts in hearing the gospel in one language and were able to write it into another language without the message getting corrupted. They used to remember whole chapters of the New Testament.

And when the time came to add these into the Bible, they translated it into Greek. And of those Greek manuscripts, we have preserved approx. 5600+ copies today with us. Just not that, we also have kept approx. 10,000+ copies of the Latin manuscripts with us.

They are all in historical archives.

Any error in one copy could easily be verified from other language manuscripts as they were all hand written. The smallest time gap between the original and the earliest copy is 50 years, and overall the time gap between all manuscripts is 50-400 years. These are great numbers.

To even top that up, we have 30,000 quotes from the early church fathers of the 1st & 2nd-century from the New Testament Bible, and you have the best case ever for the New Testament as the most well-attested document in all of history.

From these manuscripts, we can reconstruct the entire New Testament Bible many times over again.

The message that Jesus preached in Israel 2000 years ago is the exact same message that we read in our Bibles today. When you hold a Bible in your hand today, you can be certain that it is the most accurate and reliable writing in all of history.

God wanted you to be sure that the Bible you read is the most accurate Love letter He had written for you. My mind was blown with all this data.

NT Gideon Bible with Psalms and Proverbs

I was sceptical no more. All my 3 questions were now answered beautifully. My soul was in great peace. It was a personal search.

My future decisions will now be affected by the findings I explained above.

In parallel to my investigation, I was also reading the New Testament Gideon Bible with

Psalms and Proverbs. And had seen the Passion of the Christ movie almost 20 times already.

I have illustrated this diagram for you to understand how the Bible was translated over the centuries of its existence.

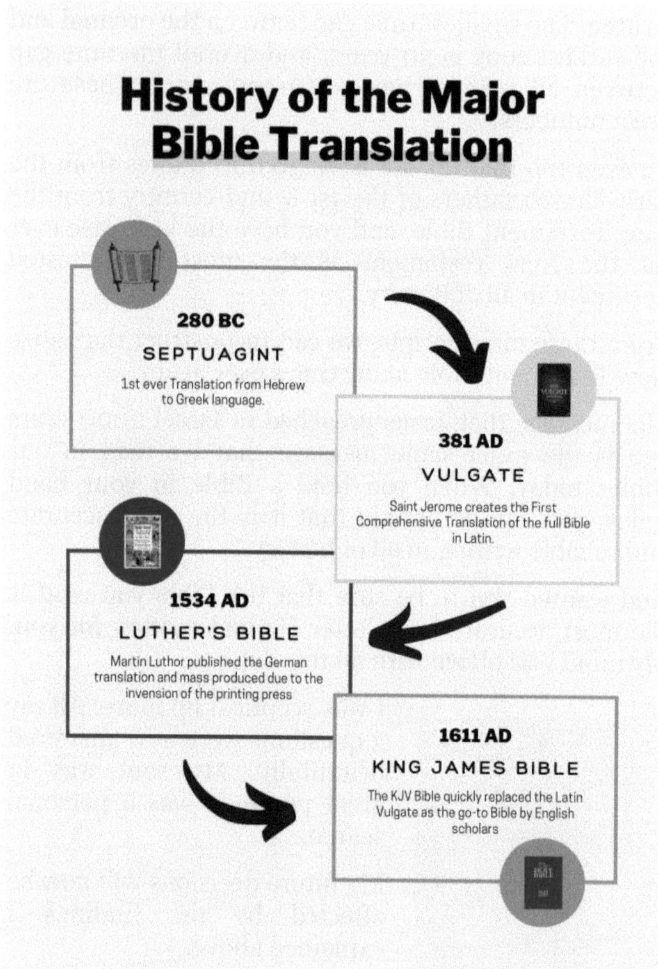

Just not history, but medical science also proves Jesus' crucifixion favourably. Every observation that was made by the disciples of Jesus and the testimonies written by the gospel writers about the medical conditions that Jesus went through during the crucifixion phase has now been medically proven to be accurate.

But I would not be covering those because it was not at the core of my research back in 2016-17. Let that be an activity for you.

Furthermore, videos of archaeological discoveries of all major biblical events make my case even stronger. I have seen countless YouTube videos of archaeologists finding the burnt cities of Sodom and Gomorrah. Discovering wheel and broken cart-shaped coral structures below the surface of the Red Sea, verifying the Exodus from Egypt led by Moses, etc...etc...

If you collect all this evidence that is out there, and few of which that I have mentioned above, and make a judiciary judgment, the court will favor the crucifixion and the resurrection of Jesus Christ.

You have to be on a truth quest and not on a happiness quest to get to the bottom. The fact that I am writing this book shows that a truth quest will always lead you to Jesus.

These are some of the books that I would recommend you read or listen to. You will get a lot more factual data and world views to think upon from these authors. Trust me, they are phenomenal in their respective fields and have great perspectives.

Seeking Allah finding Jesus by Dr. Nabeel Qureshi

The Case for Christ by Lee Strobel

Tactics by Gregory Koukl

Cold case Christianity by J Wallace

I don't have enough faith to be an Atheist by Frank Turek

Activity

Research on how accurate the medical observations in the Bible are favored by modern medicine today.

Religion

Whenever we enter into the topic of religion, things get complicated very soon. This is the only thing that people do not covet of others but love the one in which they are born. But as my guts told me, I jumped into this keeping a logical mind. But actually, this turned out to be the emotional part of the research.

Before starting with this, let me tell you about my older worldview that I had for religion. Especially for the Hindu deities.

I was born and raised in a Hindu Brahmin family. Hindus worship many gods and goddesses, but we as a family, used to worship Shirdi's Sai Baba and Maa Kali mainly since she was the goddess whom my family has been worshiping for generations.

My uncle even had constructed temples for Kali worship. As an individual, my mother used to keep weekly fasts for Santoshi Maa every Friday. All these were done to protect our house from evil.

The deities mentioned above are all Hindu gods and goddesses. There are approx. 330 million or 33 crores of these deities in Hinduism.

As my core belief, I always believed that there are many paths to go to heaven; our path was through reincarnation till all our debts/sins are paid by doing more good works than bad. I considered good deeds as respecting others, not stealing, giving money to the poor, etc...

People of other religions can attain the same by whatever they do in their respective beliefs.

I believed in Jesus, Krishna, Allah, Buddha, etc... Believed they are all different names of the same God, and all paths lead to God ultimately. People from different regions just call the same God under different names.

Oh boy, I was so wrong.

...

Since my childhood, I subconsciously knew that Hinduism was mythology. Mythology is generally described as a collection of myths, especially one belonging to a particular religious or cultural tradition. A few examples will be Greek, Egyptian, Norse, Chinese, Hindu mythologies, etc...

Even Star Wars and Harry Potter can be considered mythologies.

Coming back to Hinduism, books like the Mahabharata and Ramayana are basically a grand storybook with huge characters, each having plots and subplots. Ramayana was composed and written by Maharishi Valmiki. While Mahabharata was composed by Rishi VedVyas. As per "legend", Ganesh wrote Mahabharata, but I have got no historical evidence to prove the same.

How can a mythological character write stories in the real world? Moreover, where is the evidence of Ganesh writing the Mahabharata?

It is just believed to be so, and no further questions are asked to see if it is accurate or not. ***If I apply the same level of skepticism and scrutiny that I applied to Jesus' case and Christianity here, this argument falls apart.*** In fact, no religious worldview could stand tall other than the one about Jesus.

And as mythology goes, it is no different from J.K Rowling writing the Harry Potter Books or George Lucas creating the Star Wars mythos. It is highly possible that in 200 years from now, Star Wars may evolve into a religion. And the force and a Jedi might be considered the gods of that religion. This is how myths are born and mythologies are created.

All I want to say is there is no concrete evidence to any of the beliefs in a mythology. Whenever I read an article for proof of their historical existence, I always see people saying "It is believed". I do not want what you believe.

Just beliefs without facts are blind faith and I want no part of it. As I have previously stated, I can believe I am a 10 feet tall Chinese woman who lives on the planet Uranus and I eat moon-dust for breakfast, but my belief will not match the truth or real scenario of the real world. It would be considered delusional.

I want evidence and facts to see if something is true or not. If something is only believed to be true, it is just folklore.

Also, one key thing about any mythology/ folklore is: they are all region-based folks. Even the deities look and talk like how their culture and tradition perceive them to be. If there are any connections between deities in different myths, they are visualized in their cultural appropriation.

For example: The sun god in Hindu mythology is called Surya Devta, but the sun god in Egyptian mythology is called Ra, and has their traditional outlook in their avatars.

Sun God in Hindu Mythology

Sun God in Egyptian Mythology

Even Zeus from Greek mythology, and Thor from Norse mythology are gods of thunder. Similar concept, but different deities as per the region and its culture. Hope you are not offended by what I have written. I am just writing what I have observed. Kindly see what I am trying to say here.

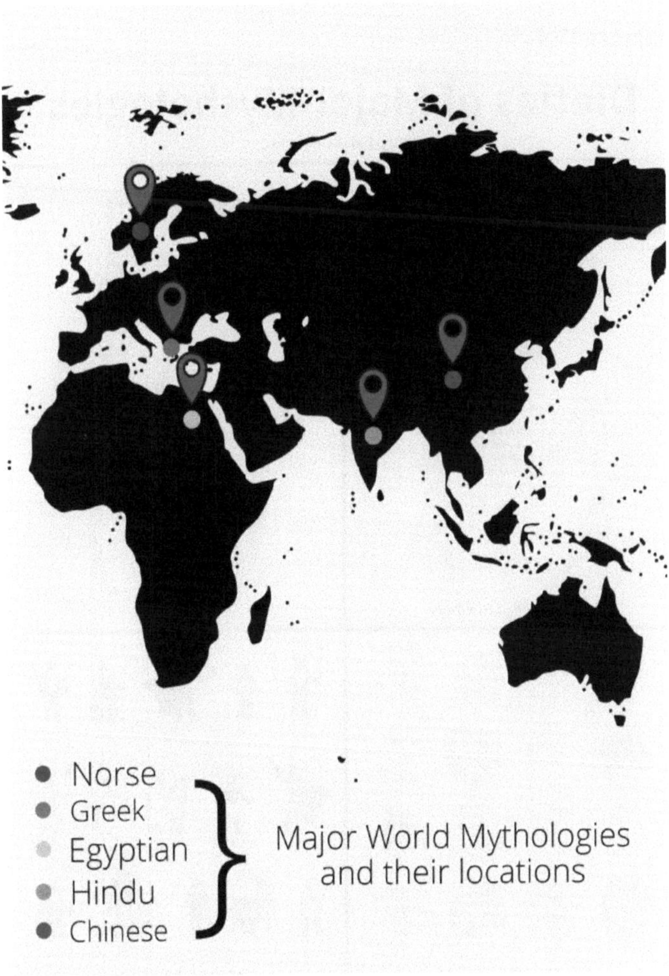
Norse
Greek
Egyptian
Hindu
Chinese
Major World Mythologies
and their locations

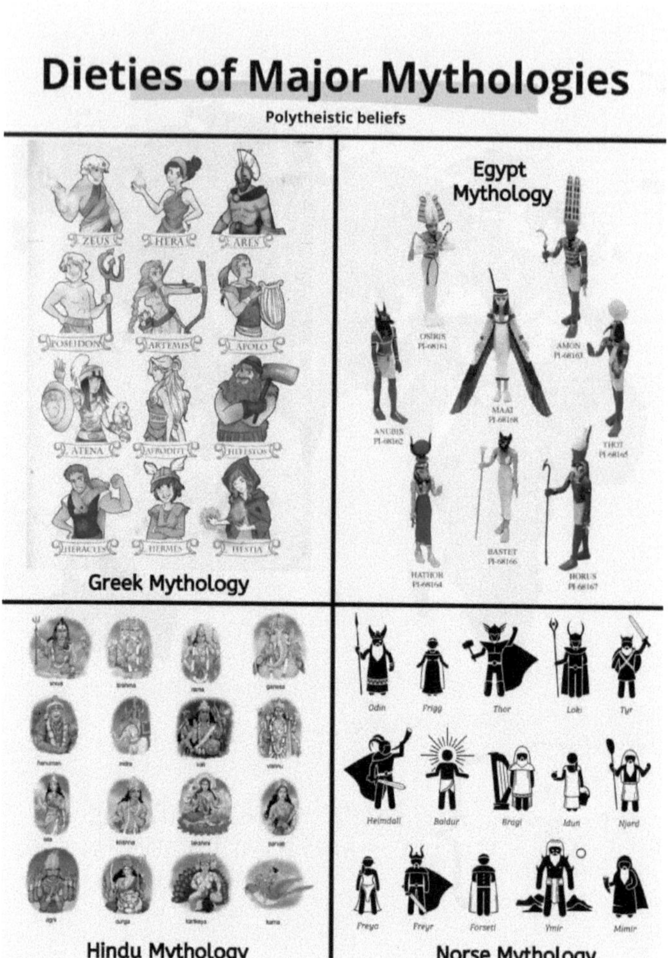

Dieties of Major Mythologies
Polytheistic beliefs
ZEUS
HERA
ARES
POSEIDON
ARTEMIS
APOLO
ATENA
HERACLES
HERMES
HESTIA
Greek Mythology
Egypt Mythology
OSIRIS
AMON
ANUBIS
MAAT
THOT
HATHOR
BASTET
HORUS
Hindu Mythology
Odin
Frigg
Thor
Loki
Tyr
Heimdall
Baldur
Bragi
Idun
Njord
Freya
Freyr
Forseti
Ymir
Mimir
Norse Mythology

"God, who made the world and everything in it, since He is Lord of heaven and earth, does **NOT** dwell in temples made with hands. Nor is He worshiped with men's hands, as though He needed anything, since He gives to all life, breath, and all things."

Acts 17:24-25

One key fact was self-evident, after keenly looking into these mythologies from all over the world, that none of them worship the GOD who created the Universe. They worship the created universe itself. Best examples would be sun, moon, thunder, cow, wind, trees, crop harvest, money, football etc... etc...

It is like me worshiping a painting which is a creation rather than the one who painted it; i.e. the painter (Creator). It is a great insult to the creator/painter.

Imagine how insulted God feels when we take stones and carve out images and start worshiping those images as our gods instead of Him. We put more trust in giant lifeless dolls and idols than we do in worshipping the Creator God. Idols will fade away, but God will never.

What can be an idol?

Well, it can be so many things to so many people. To easily define it: if you obsess about anything and dedicate most of your life actions and thoughts to it that becomes the idol of your life. It can be a person, thing, hobby, pet, sport, award, addiction, anything.

If you are a sports fan and you obsess about it. Then that sport is your idol or religion. That sport's stadium is your temple, and the best player of that sport is your god. For example:

If Football is your idol, then Pele or Maradona or Ronaldo is your god. The football stadium is your temple where you see your god. You wear a ceremonial dress jersey to worship your god.

Same goes for gyms, comic books, movie stars etc... You get the idea.

the football gods, their temple and their worshipers wearing their ceremonial outfit

What idol do you worship in your life?

The issue with Religion

Religion offers many other nice and good things, but they mostly guide us for the 80-90 years of carnal life. This guidance can easily be duplicated or replaced by self-help books and other pseudo-spiritual materials. This is the core of what I have generally understood religion to be.

Religion by and large tells us that **we can earn our way to heaven with our good deeds**. The list of deeds might change from religion to religion, but that is the core belief.

If we take good deeds for Muslims, they will be: remembering Allah from Fajr to sunrise, performing Friday and Eid prayers, being good to your parents, donating money or clothes to poor people, going to Hajj etc... All these types of deeds are more or less the same in all religions.

But what I have observed over time is that people who perform these types of deeds very efficiently, grow proud in their hearts over time. They might not realize that, but the very nature of earning righteousness on your own deeds fills your heart with pride and a superiority complex.

That brings a class system or caste system within that religion. Suddenly some people are better than others and some are worse than others. Issues like untouchability and racism start here. Ultimately, bringing violence and division among people within religions.

Therefore, repelling God out of the equation.

Satan is the god of war, confusion, and division. Whenever an ideology becomes a religion, there is bloodshed of innocent lives. Too much religion makes one violent and inter-religious issues start unfolding.

"Does any religion worship the true God who is the creator of all beings and of the universe?" A very genuine question of mine when I was in this research phase.

People go to war in the name of their religion so that their religion can spread to more lands. These religious people fight over applying their laws and are busy possessing earthly treasures as if their souls are going to live for eternity.

I feel so bad for people who die killing innocent lives in the name of their religion, who think that they will somehow inherit heaven. Truly, God who is the creator of the universe will not like to see His creation killing or fighting within themselves.

How can I boldly say that? Well, because it is written in my heart. And it is written in your heart as well. If you search for it, you will get it.

When I started researching the crusades done by the Roman Catholics, I knew that it was not from God. Jesus and war are like East and West, which never meet. The creator of this universe is anti-war and His will is not bloodshed.

One thought that we never consider is that **no one wins in a war**. That is why the kingdom of darkness loves war so much. You may think your side or your country won the war, but no, you didn't, when you look at what cost you paid for it.

Lives of good men, and women getting widowed, children losing their parents, mass graves, drained economy etc... No one wins in a war. It only feels superficially that you won.

The only one who wins in a war is the kingdom of darkness.

Kali

After all these analyses, I had huge respect for Jesus and the Bible. But still, there was something that needed to be answered for my soul. I was standing on the edge of the edge in accepting Jesus as my Lord and Savior, but was still hesitant somewhere. But where? Everything was logically right there in front of me.

Is Kali a demon goddess of destruction?

The final nail in the coffin was when I discovered the answer to this question. Kali was the chief goddess of our family for all generations and we, as a family have worshiped Maa Kali all our lives.

I have to admit that it was very emotionally difficult for me when I first heard it. It was a YouTube video from the channel, "A CALL FOR AN UPRISING".

I was swallowing all these without having any rage outburst. Being deeply offended by the details, I wanted to prove that video wrong. I started digging into the points which were shared in that video.

- Maa Kali is majorly worshiped at the ungodly hour of 3am.
- No priests but tantrics worship her.
- She is a goddess of doomsday and death. People only worship her out of fear.

I was afraid of what I may find if I dig any deeper. What might my relatives say? What may I lose?

This emotional fear was all over me. It's not that I didn't know Kali was a demon goddess. It's just that this time, I was seeing this with a different set of lenses/worldviews created by the research I did. If you find her familiar, she is the same goddess as in the movie: **Indiana Jones and the Temple of Doom.**

No doubt, all the findings that I had to do are for the 1st point. I already knew that Kali was a scary, bloodthirsty embodiment of death and destruction. Personally, I used to fear her since my childhood. Especially because of her violent poses as seen in the pictures.

I have visited the Hindu pilgrimage centre of Chinnamasta which is located in Rajrappa, Ramgarh district of Jharkhand, India. Chinnamasta is one of many forms of Kali who is worshiped mainly among tantrics.

I always used to be very scared of her the most, out of all Kali avatars, since she is completely nude and her head is cut off, spilling blood. It is a very disturbing image to see as a child.

When I asked my mother why we pray and worship Kali, she gave me exactly the same answer as claimed in that YouTube video.

My mother said she fears that if all the scheduled rituals are not done properly, Kali might get angry at our family and something bad might happen because of that. All the poojas and worship was more out of fear in order to keep Kali pleased.

Just not Kali, my mother worshiped all other Hindu deities, not out of pure devotion but mainly out of fear, i.e., to keep the well-being of our Family.

Out of my personal experience, Kali is not a protector of evil but is actually a mafia who takes ritualistic ransoms from us to keep us safe from herself and other Mafias like her. To make it simple, Kali is a mafia who protected us from other Mafias if our worship offerings were pleasing to her.

The possibility of her being a demon was not that far-fetched. If I look back to 25 years of my existence, I cannot remember any good thing happening to us by worshiping her anyway. It has always been fear-mongering to do this or that; else you may face the consequences of this type of relationship. Basically a threat.

Coming to the other point of the hour of Kali's worship, I needed to dig for information from Demonology.

The Devil's Hour (3am)

I have seen Kali being worshiped at night at 3am by ***tantrics*** in Dakshineswar Temple, Kolkata. I always wondered that it was quite an odd time to worship anything godly.

According to studies on Demons (Demonology), demonic spirits will do exactly the opposite of what Jesus stood for. That is their very nature, i.e., to oppose GOD and His will in every possible way.

Jesus gave up His spirit in the afternoon of 3pm, which in turn is now known as the most "godly" hour.

And exactly 12 hours later, i.e., at 3am, is the most "ungodly" hour. At this time all kinds of demonic activities increase. In hindsight, while demons are weakest at 3pm, they are strongest at 3am because they are opposite to whatever Jesus is related to.

It has also been observed that 3am is the time when maximum witchcraft rituals and occult sacrifices take place. Apparently, the fact that "nobody" can watch them makes them more powerful. It all relates to the very nature of demons.

It is also quite noticeable in Hollywood horror movies. All demonic activities start at 3-4am.

Hollywood horror movies showing demonic activities at 3 am

Coming to the third point, tantrics have always worshiped Kali. A tantric is an Indian occultist and they practice occult & mysticism and do black magic. But now you know what black magic or witchcraft is. Similar to witchcraft, they do all sorts of evil rituals on dead bodies and meditate in cemeteries. Not a good place to be for godly people.

They also cast spells and use them to solve their problems or their clients, who pay them for their needs.

Just not that, but the biggest devotee of Kali: Ramakrishna used to also spend a lot of time in cemeteries and in deep spiritual meditation. He always used to be in a trans-like phase (lost and clueless), as if he was possessed by spirits.

Now, because of all my findings, what most people see as a goddess, I was witnessing a demon who demands worship.

This is more evident when you see Ramakrishna making the devil's horn sign.

As per my earlier explanation from the 'Symbols' chapter, devil's horns are used as a curse symbol. You can see devil worshipers flashing it deliberately. It would completely make sense if Ramakrishna flashed them as he worshiped Kali. See these images below.

There are multiple instances caught on record where Ramakrishna is making the devil's horns. Photographs were rarely taken at the time when Ramakrishna lived (1836-86). But here I have got 2 photos where he is showing the devil's horns hand sign blatantly.

Ramakrishna was not in a heavy metal rock band, so he didn't mean that hand sign to be the rock and roll sign. It was back in the 1800s in India; rock and roll or hard rock was not born yet.

It cannot get any more obvious than this. Wake up guys, if not already.

I was now completely convinced of who Jesus was. This was the last domino of my scepticism. Had no other way than to walk on my discovered path. The path which is always the narrow road. The path which led me to Jesus' Kingdom.

“Enter by the narrow gate; for wide is the gate and broad is the way that leads to destruction, and there are many who go in by it. Because **NARROW** is the gate and difficult is the way which leads to life, and there are few who find it.”

Matthew 7:13-14

The Good Shepherd

My Failure

Till this point in my journey, I had a plan to excel at a certain career path, and was actively pursuing that. This job was mainly to get into the field in which I had a bachelor's degree. According to me, if my plan had come through, it would have been a life-altering event for me at that time.

Unfortunately, things didn't turn out the way they should have, and all my time and efforts pursuing that field and career were over. It was a very hurtful experience for my soul. After all, I had invested 2 years of my life pursuing it and 4 years in college for the degree. 6 years in total.

Whenever I had planned anything in my life a certain way, it has never turned out that way. Rather the opposite. This is what happens when you keep planning for future years intensively and miss out on signs that it's a red flag zone.

I had planned my entire future on the basis of this career path. But once my chances failed, all my wannabe plans collapsed, like a house of cards would.

These were parallel events going on in my life apart from the research. After a dark 2015, followed by this failure in 2017, I really felt like a complete loser. It was definitely the lowest point of my life.

The Open Invitation

Now we are entering into the fun part of my testimony. Whenever I hear other people's testimony of how they were saved, I get blown away that each and every believer gets a unique revelation from God for their salvation. God always comes with new ideas, a custom made salvation plan to reveal Himself to those who want to truly know Him, tailored just for that precious soul.

I can guarantee that no two believers can come and proclaim that their testimonies are exactly the same.

With my broken dreams and plans, one night I was just wondering about my life and destiny. My head used to be blank, and that's why I used to have many sleepless nights during that time period overthinking all my past life decisions. Everything was out of my control, and only God, (if He exists) could give me an answer to this mess. I needed to pray.

For the 1st time in my life, I didn't know which God to pray to, or even if there was a God, to begin with. I was not at all thinking logically but had a lot of doubt, anger, and grief in my heart. Trust me; it is a huge burden to carry. This loser didn't know the purpose of his life and needed a plan, and I just hoped that if there is a creator out there who has created me, He can help me if I pray.

The first domino of my faith journey was about to fall.

So I woke up from my bed, went to a lonely part of my house, raised my hand as a gesture of surrender, and humbly made this unique prayer:

"This prayer is for you who is the creator of this world. I don't know who you are. You can be Allah, Buddha, Krishna, or Jesus.

I don't care. If you exist and if you love me, then reveal yourself to me. You have created me and this universe; the least you can do is talk to me. I am in great pain.

This is an open invitation to you. I would love to get to know you and build a relationship with you.

I am all ears for you."

These were the genuine words that I could come up with and spoke them earnestly. This was more of a conversation than a prayer: **An open invitation** to God to enter my life. After all, if God is the one who has scientifically and mathematically created this universe and its complexities, then He could easily crack my prayer.

I don't have to go to temples or mosques or churches or anywhere to make God hear me. We don't need to talk and cry in front of lifeless idols.

Even if I had prayed this prayer in a filthy toilet, He would listen to me just as someone who is sitting in a clean room, has taken a bath, and wearing clean clothes. This new mind-set of praying was new to me. It was awesome.

Activity

Go to a secret or more private part of your home where you can pray alone secretly, and pray the exact prayer that I prayed.

Within a period of 2-3 months, I started seeing some weird dreams. In one such dream, I was trapped in a dark tunnel. That darkness had a personality of its own and was threatening to harm me if I left them. When I turned around, there was no one but an endless path of darkness. It was scolding me, trying its best to keep me with itself. And in the front was light: The tunnel opening. I knew I had to get out of there and the more I kept going ahead, the voices kept fading away.

The light kept getting bigger and bigger and the darkness kept fading away as if it was way scared of that light which I was following.

That was the time I knew it was Jesus. No one told me that. I just knew it. Strange right. The Shepherd finally came for His sheep. One who was lost in this world finally reunites with his Creator. Many nightmares like that happened, but I don't remember any of them. Just this one.

No other God but Jesus showed up. I repeatedly kept praying the same prayer for a week, but it was only Jesus who cared for me to show up.

He didn't appear in a vision or dream or so, but via other mediums. I have felt His presence through many YouTube channels/videos, sermon preaching, books, etc.., slowly changing my heart and growing His seed in me. Now I can call God my Father. He is not distant from me anymore.

One day after a good praise and thanksgiving prayer, I saw a YouTube video as a recommendation on top of my page. That was the very 1st video I saw for the day, and it was a long message from my Heavenly Father. It went like this:

My child, you may not know me, but I know everything about you. - Psalm 139:1

I know when you sit down and when you rise up. - Psalm 139:2

I am familiar with all your ways. - Psalm 139:3

Even the very hairs on your head are numbered. - Matthew 10:29-31

For you were made in My image. - Genesis 1:27

In me, you live and move and have your being. For you are My offspring. - Acts 17:28

I knew you even before you were conceived - Jeremiah 1:4-5

I chose you when I planned creation. - Ephesians 1:11-12

You were not a mistake, for all your days are written in My book. - Psalm 139:15-16

I determined the exact time of your birth and where you would live. - Acts 17:26

You are fearfully and wonderfully made. - Psalm 139:14

I knit you together in your mother's womb. - Psalm 139:13

And brought you forth on the day you were born. - Psalm 71:6

I have been misrepresented by those who don't know Me. - John 8:41-44

I am not distant and angry but am the complete expression of love. - 1st John 4:16

And it is My desire to lavish My love on you. Simply because you are My child and I am your Father. - 1st John 3:1

I offer you more than your earthly father ever could. Matthew 7:11

For I am the perfect Father. Matthew 5:48

Every good gift that you receive comes from My hand. James 1:17

For I am your provider and I meet all your needs. Matthew 6:31-33

My plans for your future have always been filled with hope. Jeremiah 29:11

Because I love you with an everlasting love. Jeremiah 31:3

My thoughts towards you are as countless as the sand on the seashore. Psalm 139:17-18:

And I rejoice over you with singing. Zephaniah 3:17

I will never stop doing good to you. Jeremiah 32:40

For you are My treasured possession. Exodus 19:5

I desire to establish you with all My heart and all My soul. Jeremiah 32:41

And I want to show you great and marvelous things. Jeremiah 33:3

If you seek Me with all your heart, you will find Me. Deuteronomy 4:29

Delight in Me and I will give you the desires of your heart. Psalm 37:4

For it is I who gave you those desires. Philippians 2:13

I am able to do more for you than you could possibly imagine. Ephesians 3:20

For I am your greatest encouragement. 2nd Thessalonians 2:16-17

I am also the Father who comforts you in all your troubles. 2nd Corinthians 1:3-4

When you are brokenhearted, I am close to you. Psalm 34:18

As a shepherd carries a lamb, I have carried you close to My heart. Isaiah 40:11

One day, I will wipe away every tear from your eyes. And I will take away all the pain you have suffered. Revelation 21:3-4

I am your Father, and I love you even as I love My Son, Jesus. John 17:23

For in Jesus, My love for you is revealed. John 17:26

He is the exact representation of My being. Hebrews 1:3

He came to demonstrate that I am for you, not against you. Romans 8:31

And to tell you that I am not counting your sins. Jesus died so that you and I could be reconciled. 2 Corinthians 5:18-19

His death was the ultimate expression of My love for you. 1st John 4:10

I gave up everything I loved that I might gain your love. Romans 8: 31-32

If you receive the gift of My Son Jesus, you receive Me. 1st John 2:23

And nothing will ever separate you from My love again. Romans 8:38-39

Come home and I will throw the biggest party heaven has ever seen. Luke 15:7

I have always been Father, and will always be Father. Ephesians 3:14-15

But, Will you be My child? John 1:12-13

I am waiting for you. Luke 15:11-32

This was a love letter from God. He loves me and He is crazy about me. Finally, on 10th April 2017, I was baptized by His Holy Spirit. I accepted Jesus Christ as my Lord and Savior in my heart, and have never turned back since then. However, the baptism of water came years later on 20th January 2021, just a few weeks before the completion of this book.

It's a Relationship, not a Religion

I understood that this was no religion but a very personal and intimate relationship with God. I was not a religious Christian by any stretch, but a sinner who had accepted his sins and was ready to repent to the one who had paid a ransom for my sins. Jesus had paid my unpayable fine through His blood. I am now a born-again soul in Christ Jesus.

I felt an overwhelming peace entering my heart which cannot be explained. This event changed my life thereafter. Not just mine, but the life of my entire family. I debated with my sister, and after a few long days of reasoning, she too gave her life to Jesus. So did my mother and my father.

God invited my whole family into His Kingdom and now we all have gladly accepted His Free Gift of Salvation. We are not religious Christians, but born again in His Holy Spirit.

It is really amazing to me what God will do and how God will pursue us. It does not matter where you are born, which religion you belong to, or what race you came from. His love will not quit on you. It is not an accident that you came reading this page of this book. Know this thing for sure: Jesus loves you more than your mother or father ever could. He will never leave you nor forsake you.

God is all-loving to us as a Father, but He is also the true Justice-keeper. In the eyes of God, any and everything which is not connected to Him is sin. It does not matter if you steal a pen or huge sums of money from a bank; ***a sin is a sin,*** and He will judge accordingly.

If He forgives all our sins just like that, then there is no justice to be done. If God shows only mercy, that will make Him an awful Judge. So God, as a true Judge, cannot let sin go unpunished without payment or fine. Justice and penalty for the sins of the whole world are required to be paid somehow.

But at the same time, God is all loving and considers us as His children. As a loving Father wants all His children to be saved, so God came up with an awesome plan.

He gave up His most - most - most beloved and only Son Jesus. And Jesus, with His free will accepted whatever God wanted Him to do. That is why God exalted His name, so that the whole world shall bow down and shall profess that 'Jesus Christ is Lord'. - Philippians 2:10

This is the very same reason why Satan made only Jesus' name a cuss word in this sinful world, because that name is most favored by God and people are blessed through His holy name.

God has never created religion but instead wants a deep personal relationship with us so that we can call

Him Abba Father, and depend on Him for our everyday requirements. He is not a master who just gives rules to His followers, but rather He is a loving Father who has adopted us and has washed our sins by the Blood of Christ.

It's a relationship and not a religion. If it were a religion, then I would be very comfortable with Hinduism itself. There was no requirement for me to give up all the *bhogs* and *prasads* and go through intense criticism from my relatives about following Jesus.

Can you imagine, God who is called "*Malik*" or master by the rest of the world, Him, we can call as our own Father! What an inheritance and privilege anyone can have through Jesus Christ!

Jesus is our Soul Insurance

Activity

If you think that you are a good person and your morals are perfect, then answer these questions below honestly to understand why you need Jesus only for your salvation.

- Have you ever stolen anything in your life? Yes/No
- Have you ever lied in your life? Yes/No
- Have you ever lusted over worldly materials? Yes/No

- Have you taken God's name as a cuss word? Yes/No
- Are you a good person? Yes/No

If your answer was 'Yes' to any of these questions, you have sinned and have fallen short of God's glory because you have to be 100% sinless to enter His Kingdom. You need Jesus' salvation.

A Brother in Christ: Ray Comfort from Living Waters, asks these questions to make people realize how flawed and sinful we are according to God's standards.

I pray that whoever is reading this book, may come to know the Lord Jesus Christ and be saved. May His Holy Spirit build His temple in your heart with praise, joy, and thanksgiving.

The Attack

The kingdom of darkness hates when someone starts walking away from their grasp. Especially those who newly entered Jesus' kingdom.

So when I came to Christ, all evil spirits got a note of it. As if in their headquarters, a big picture of mine was posted in their Most Wanted section with a good bounty reward on me.

Spiritual attacks were bound to happen. Before continuing ahead, just know that demons attack in many ways. They attack via nightmares, physical harm, or direct possession of the human body.

My attacks were physical harm and nightmares. If you are a true believer, you know exactly what I am talking about.

Starting with nightmares, I used to have, on average of 3 nightmares a week and that continued for 2 months after my salvation. Mostly it would be someone chasing after me. And in a few, I would be fighting someone or something off me which would grab me and won't let me go, etc...

I was actively reading my Bible and was simultaneously listening to some great spirit-filled Christian content online, and eventually, I came to know about my Authority because of what Christ has conquered through His blood. As Jesus followers, we are commanded to rebuke demons, heal the sick, and much more.

Read Matthew 10:8.

“Heal the sick, raise the dead, cleanse the lepers, cast out demons. Freely you receive, freely give.”

Matthew 10:8

Apart from nightmare attacks, I used to get some physical attacks too. Nothing very violent, but definitely they were supernatural.

At times I used to feel a sudden burning pain in my back. Upon inspection, I would find that there were long scratches, as if something or someone had run sharp claws over my back.

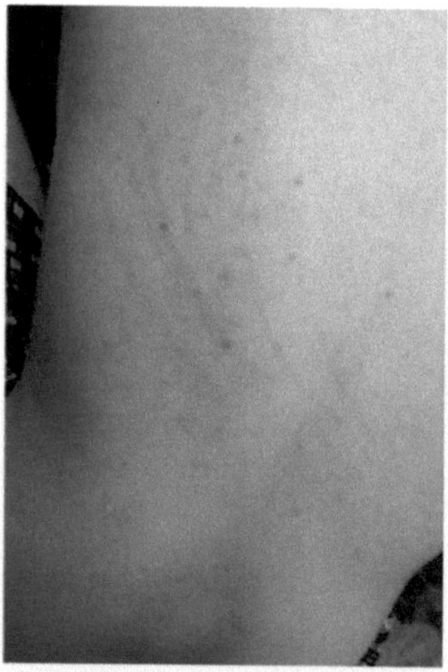

My back with scratches

At first, I tried to find a rational explanation for this. I own cats and if there are any scratches on my body, it would be by them.

But even my cat would not drag their claws all over my back without me knowing about it. I never knew when I got these scratches. It was only felt after it started to burn in pain.

They were especially felt at night during sleep.

Something even weirder than that happened right around the same time period. I was a recent Born Again Christian and had an argument with my mother over a small issue. I went to sleep that night with a heavy heart, filled with unforgiveness over the matter with my mom. A perfect opportunity that the kingdom of darkness took to attack me.

I woke up the next morning witnessing a nightmare where a creepy Joker like monster was after my life and I kept running from him. Once I woke up, I was stuck in my bed, paralyzed. I was not able to move my hands, legs or my head. As if an invisible weight was over me. My heart was immediately filled with terror.

I knew it was a demon trying to get me because of last night's argument and unforgiveness that I had against my mother.

As if unknowingly, I had rented a small real estate of my soul to the spirit of un-forgiveness, and this demon was the new tenant who came to live on that plot. But the entire real estate of my soul has been recently acquired by Jesus, and such un-forgiveness, if continued, will allow this evil tenant to capture the entire real estate, taking me away from my savior and making my soul more miserable.

The Holy Spirit revealed this to me at that terrifying moment, in the state of that paralysis. I immediately forgave my mother in my heart and asked Jesus to take over this situation.

I wanted to scream 'save me Jesus' but I was so terrified that no voice came out of my scream. It was more of a muted version of a scream.

The courage to do all this came from the Holy Spirit. Within seconds after making that prayer, that heaviness was lifted off me and I was able to move. I felt like a character from a typical horror movie.

As that spirit left me, I knew it went under my bed because soon as I sat up right from the paralysis, my entire bed started shaking as if I was in the middle of an earthquake. I slept once again because I didn't want to jump from a shaking bed. I started praying again.

After a minute or two, the shaking stopped.

All these unrealistic sounding things actually happened to me. Seriously, I cannot make these things up.

" For we wrestle not against flesh and blood, but against principalities, against powers, against the rulers of the darkness of this world, against spiritual wickedness in high places."

Ephesians 6:12.

But these issues were nothing to the awesome revelations I was getting from God at the same-time. Whatever I have shared in this book is God's revelation to me, and now, to you as well.

The Revelations

After spending a good time knowing God and being in His presence via praise, prayer, singing, and thanksgiving, He revealed a lot of His heart to me. Jesus came to live under God's law to achieve righteousness or holiness as a man. As a mortal, common human being like you and me.

He had to do that because God demanded a level of righteousness from Him; no other human could offer it to God. Ever. So Jesus, with His everlasting love and free will, said He would become a man and would live to be born under the law, and would live it perfectly to achieve the level of righteousness, God demands from us humans.

Jesus lived under the law as a human for the humans, thus becoming the ultimate High Priest whose life is to be imitated by anyone who follows Jesus.

On the cross, Jesus made the biggest exchange offer ever known to humanity. He took our sins and exchanged it for His righteousness. That whoever does this exchange will have everlasting life through His righteousness. That is the entire deal behind being Born Again.

And therefore, Jesus's way of living is now our ideal standard of living for whatever number of years we ought to live on Earth.

He also revealed a lot of personal and general promises to me. Most of the general promises are all written in the Word of God: the Bible. But apart from that, these are a few things He has taught me.

Why is Blood so important?

As a newcomer to faith, the concept of the Blood of Jesus washing all our sins was a little confusing to me. I didn't understand how and why the blood of all things was considered by God as the payment of sins for all humanity, past, present and future.

In biology, Blood is sort of a delivery agent that not only gives your cells Oxygen and Food nutrients, but is also the one that takes the garbage out like urea and carbon dioxide out of each body cell.

Blood also fights infections, and carries hormones around the body, i.e., taking care of the cells with all of their problems.

I don't know about you, but the function of blood resembles Jesus to me. He didn't just give us grace, joy, and salvation, but also took away our sins and scars. He protects our souls from all demonic attacks too.

That is why the Blood of Jesus is the only payment God accepts for eternally forgiving our sins. Trust me; the Blood of Jesus is so complete that no unclean spirit can ever bear its presence.

The perfect and only medicine against sin.

How can Jesus' blood wash away all of our sins - Past, Present, and Future?

All living organisms of this world have some sort of value and importance that they are classified as. Jesus is at the top of that value chain. His blood has the highest of values that there can be. Well, let me explain this with an analogy.

If I were to classify a mosquito, a puppy, and a human, according to their value, how would I do so? We kill dozens of mosquitoes every day. Are you getting arrested for that? No right. OK, let's increase the stakes a little bit higher.

Let's kill a puppy (hypothetically), you might not get arrested but people in your locality will definitely start maintaining distance from you, and animal rights activists might criticize you, online and offline, but that might not affect you negatively for the long term.

Now, let's up the game. Try killing an adult human (hypothetically). The stakes have increased a lot all of a sudden. Now, you will be guilty of a serious crime, i.e. Murder.

Back when you killed dozens of mosquitoes, no one cared about those lives. You were not called a serial killer. But suddenly when the value of life was increased from a mosquito to an adult human, you might get hanged for it, or at least a life sentence in prison.

The act of murder didn't change, but the value of life, who was murdered definitely changed. Now raise the stake ultimately to God, who entered His own creation as a man, lived a sinless life, and died after brutal torture on a cross for our sins; now you tell me, what value does His death and His blood play.

The Holy Spirit cleared all my earlier misconceptions on what I knew from the 1st chapter of this book. The British East India Company wanted to rule the world in the name of the Queen of England and not in the name of Jesus Christ.

That so-called company wanted to loot all of their colonies, of which India was also a part. It was the Christian missionaries who saw an opportunity to preach the gospel to us and started opening hospitals, schools and orphanage centers to help all and share Jesus with the meek and the poor.

Why does God allow Evil to flourish on Earth?

This is one of the most common questions I have seen being asked by everyone on the internet. How come a good God who loves us can allow evil to go rampant on Earth without stopping it? I too, had this question on my mind. The answer to which is very simple. It's **Free Will**.

Free Will

You see, Free Will is a double-edged sword. It can cut both ways. God, in his all lovingness, has granted each one of us the free will to do what we want. Even we have the power to reject God's love with our free will. That is why Heaven and Hell exist. God loves us enough to respect your decision. Even your decision to depart from Him.

Heaven simply means to stay in the presence of God. And Hell is separation from God that we freely choose because we hate God and His ways. Hell lacks all those things that God has created to sustain life.

Out of our own Free Will, we have proudly selected sin, addiction, hatred, war, lust, envy, anger. Out of our materialistic pride we have denounced being called as a child of God, and instead take pride in calling ourselves children of the devil.

It is out of our free will, many have chosen to get drunk and do all sorts of evil with our fellow brothers. So let me ask one question to you:

Why do we continue doing evil with our free will and reject God?

Whenever one cheats, murders, rapes, or does any other form of evil to another human, we hurt God. Remember that every person is created in the image of God. You may not want that, but that is how you are made.

But this does not mean that all evil will go unpunished. God is the Ultimate Judge, and the ultimate Justice will come upon the evildoers. Doesn't matter if you have stolen a pencil or a car, you will be judged on stealing accordingly, because with free will comes the accountability of your decisions and the consequences for it.

Our carnal life is like a speck of dust as compared to eternity. This carnal world we are living in is degrading day by day, so instead of following the world you focus on God and all your atrocities will be washed out. It happened to me. It can surely happen with you too.

My request to you is to choose God with your free will, as I have done.

"But He was wounded for our transgressions, He was bruised for our iniquities; The chastisement for our peace was upon Him, And by His stripes, we are healed."

Isaiah 53:5

All of Creation is made in God's image

This is one of the greatest revelations God has given me. He is an artist who loves to create everything in His own image. So logically, all things that you see around you must have the signature of the Creator. Everything is made in trinities because God is a triune God. **The Father, the Son, and the Holy Spirit.**

This diagram explains it best. Check this out.

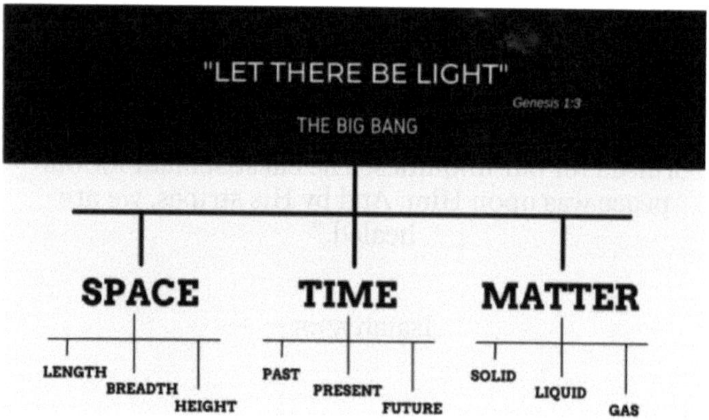

When the Universe was formed, God created it out of nowhere based on 3 basic things: Time, Space, and Matter (Triune). Many scientists call it the Big Bang. Even time, space, and matter were subdivided into three more categories. They are also individually triune.

1. Space into length, breadth, and height (Triune).
2. Time into past, present, and future (Triune again), and
3. Matter into solid, liquid, and gas (Triune again).

So now we have got the trinity of trinity creation.

When I see the universe designed to such accuracy, it amazes me how finely tuned each and everything has to be in order for Earth to inhabit life.

The best part is that many physical constants must be finely-tuned or just right in order to continue life to sustain on this planet. Earth is equipped with a pair of magnetic poles which protect us from harmful solar flares from the Sun. The planet Jupiter acts like a giant vacuum cleaner in the solar system, protecting Earth from any deadly asteroids.

God has not only created us but has thought of all sorts of protective measures to keep our world really safe.

And the amazing fact is, even the tiniest particles ever called atoms and our existence as human beings are triune by nature as well. Study the diagram below. If this is not called perfect design, what is?

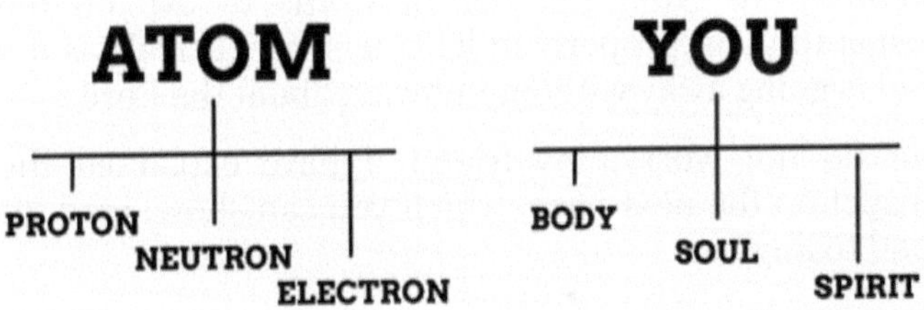

I studied about the triune nature of humans from the book: *Spirit, Soul and Body by Andrew Wommack*. You must definitely add it to your to-read list.

Sharing the Word

The more you are convinced in the Gospel on a factual and logical basis, the more it will be easy for you to speak to sceptics. I have seen many Christians who have blind faith in God and Jesus; i.e. a faith without any facts supporting its core.

When they are bombarded with tough questions regarding the authenticity of the Bible or who Jesus is, their faith and worldview gets shaken. It crumbles down.

Doubt has now entered their minds. But you, do your proper research, get all the facts right, and now keep this book and the other resources that I shared as a piece of evidence with you at all times.

That is why this book was written and published. Have this spiritual weapon for all who are rationally seeking Jesus as well as those who are already following Him. Feel free to use this weapon against the kingdom of darkness.

Over time, I have faced huge problems in articulating the good news of Jesus Christ in the right words. Many times, when people are hostile, in a hurry, or are skeptics, we often run out of words to explain the gospel to them properly in its true sense. It feels as if a soul is going away without knowing about the Lord.

But do not worry, my friend. I have explained the Gospel on the next page, which you can show, read, or send to anyone.

Here it goes:

Those who have ears to hear:
Here is the Good News of Salvation.

We all have sinned by rebelling against God through our pride, lies, lust, hatred, anger, etc.. and have fallen short of His glory.

Regardless of that, **GOD** so loved each one of us that He gave His only son (Jesus) to die for our sins on the cross.

But ***Jesus rose again***, defeating death. So that whoever believes in His perfect sacrifice can have a personal relationship with God and enter His presence for eternity.

Not by following religious rules and rituals, but solely depending on Jesus's love, grace and His

FREE GIFT OF SALVATION

earned through His **Blood**.

"Oh give thanks to the Lord; call upon His name; make known His deeds among the peoples!"

1 Chronicles 16:8

Your Soul Insurance

We are just temporary wanderers in this world - the truth, which should be evident to everyone, but we find some excuse to deny seeing it.

Our human body is a rented house and our soul just rents it for 80 - 90 years, depending on how long we live. This rented body grows up since our soul arrives to check-in them to stay.

The 1st stage is nine months long in your mother's womb. Then, the 2nd stage begins outside of it. In the 2nd stage, your rented body grows from infancy to childhood. From childhood to adulthood. And finally, from adulthood to old age.

One is very fortunate if they have lived to become old. Due to many reasons like accidents, deadly diseases, pandemics etc.., many die untimely deaths. Sometimes, the eviction notice on the rental property comes very soon. Sooner than anyone can expect. God can call a few of us early.

But many die because of the choices of their free will. A chain smoker who leaves his rental property does that because of his smoking addiction. The same goes for drug addicts and drunkards. You get the idea.

Many of you who are reading this don't think about these things this way. I know that because I was like you for 25 years. I consider that Jesus saved my soul at an early age and He is offering to save your soul as well. The only one who can guarantee your soul insurance is Jesus. Read John 14:6.

"My home is in Heaven. I am just traveling through this world."

Billy Graham

Tomorrow is not promised to anyone, my friend. You are a unique creation of God. As per the letter you read earlier, He knew us when we were in our mother's womb. The message I want to tell you is that, do not worry about the 80 or 90 years of your carnal life. Our lives are like a puff in the air, that appears for a little time, and then vanishes away. - James 4:14

But think about the eternity of your soul instead. There will be no one like you ever in the existence of time. Even if you have a twin sibling who is identical to you. They have different souls. That is why your fingerprints and retinas are not identical.

As humans, we over-plan our vacations, places to visit, tickets to buy, hotels to choose from. So much planning, but for how many days? For a few days, a week maybe.

But these same people completely neglect where their souls will go after they die. Why do you not think or plan for your eternity as well?

As per ourworldindata.org, nearly 58.39 million people died around the world in 2019, and it is not even counting the pandemic death counts for 2020. Get your soul eternally insured through Lord Jesus today.

I started my soul-searching journey after pondering the question of where my soul would go after my death. I hope that after reading this book, you ponder upon the same question as well. Where will my soul be after I leave this world?

Do think about this for a moment; you do not have to take my research into account. You do your own unbiased research and genuinely ask God to guide you. We all have got our free will.

I hope reading through my testimony has helped you in some shape or form.

Thank you for reading my story.

Our time on Earth is limited, research for yourself and make a wise decision today.

Do not depart from this world without knowing Christ

CHANNELS THAT HELPED

YouTube

Acts17Apologetics

Michael Chriswell

Almas Jacob

Truthunedited

Living Waters

Cross Examined

A CALL FOR AN UPRISING

Cold-Case Christianity

BibleProject

Kent Hovind

A special thank you to all of these channels. Without their videos, this testimony would be incomplete. You guys are doing Lord's work. Keep at it.

The King is coming
Soon

Notes

Notes

Notes

Notes

9 789393 388537

Printed by Libri Plureos GmbH in Hamburg,
Germany